BASICS IN
JAZZ
ARRANGING

PARIS RUTHERFORD

HAL•LEONARD® CORPORATION

7777 W. BLUEMOUND RD. P.O. BOX 13819 MILWAUKEE, WI 53213

ISBN: 978-1-4803-4069-5

In Australia Contact:
Hal Leonard Australia Pty. Ltd.
4 Lentara Court
Cheltenham, Victoria, 3192 Australia
Email: ausadmin@halleonard.com.au

Printed in the U.S.A.

First Edition

Visit Hal Leonard Online at
www.halleonard.com

CONTENTS

PREFACE

Writing music is a fascinating journey, one that should always reap emotional profits both for the composer/arranger and for those that perform and enjoy the music. Whether in a classroom setting or individual study, *Basics in Jazz Arranging* is a guide through the essential elements of successful writing, chapter by chapter, as follows:

1. Making profitable and efficient use of one's time and creativity is the "name of the game."

2. Having chosen a tune to arrange, its melody must be treated sensitively, whatever the style, for the rest of the journey to be worthwhile. After deciding upon a performing ensemble, we select the best key and style and outline the project so that our time is well spent.

3. Harmony then enters the picture, serving carefully to enhance the product, and individualize our work. (This is a sensitive issue, since over-writing will compromise our work.)

4. Composition is always present, whether in one's original music or in the process of arranging. When we compose, we then arrange; when we arrange other composers' music, we use the compositional process to enhance the product without altering the composers' original music.

5. Whatever the size and makeup of the performing ensemble, we search for the best idiomatic treatment of the music we arrange and/or orchestrate, including our own compositions.

6. We then focus on giving the rhythm section (small or large) the information they need for the best possible performance. Having spent time listening to great recordings, we become more and more sensitive to the awakening of creativity in our own minds.

7. And finally, we make sure that the written product is accurate, with as professional an appearance as possible. Once a written project leaves our venue, it represents us forever.

Basics in Jazz Arranging is an outgrowth of my work at the University of North Texas, where for three decades I taught jazz arranging classes and labs varying in size. In the first semester, for which *Basics* was the assigned text, classes ranged in size from 50 to 70 students. Most of these were performers who had no idea that they could write good music. The great majority of these students left the class succeeding as writers. I am pleased and honored to hear every year from a large number who now compose and arrange as part of their career.

Writing music is indeed a fascinating journey. I hope that *Basics in Jazz Arranging* helps to send you on your way to success in this area!

CHAPTER ONE
GETTING STARTED

Choosing a Tune to Arrange

The first step in arranging is choosing the right tune, or becoming thoroughly acquainted with one assigned or requested. If the choice is yours:

- Select your tune from the standard repertoire. **Standards** are so labeled because they have proven themselves through hundreds of arrangements, both in live performances and recordings. See the list of great standards on page 6, grouped by their song forms.

- Select a tune in which you feel the room to express some ideas of your own. Original rhythms for tunes written with lyrics will tend to feel awkward when the lyrics are removed. By adjusting the melodic rhythms according to the style of your chart, you have already begun the arranging process.

- Be careful to avoid extremes in tempo, rhythmic complexity, and harmonic complexity while you are still new to arranging. Succeeding with simplicity is important.

As you search through printed collections and CDs, spend time listening to great recordings in the style you have chosen. Tune your ears from the outside in.

Printed Music Sources

Sheet Music
Sheet music is the descriptive term for single retail copies of published music. Though single copies are seldom sold now in the jazz arena, the term "sheet music" continues to describe the most basic and earliest version of a tune. This term, though, should not be confused with **lead sheet**, which is a one-line copy of only the melody (lead line) with chord symbols (above the melody) and lyrics (below the melody), when they exist.

Real Books
Real Books are those published volumes containing a wealth of jazz standards, as well as tunes in other styles. Their contents continue to be updated and upgraded, and are available both online and in music stores. *The Real Book* is published by Hal Leonard Corporation and by Sher Music. There are also online versions of these materials available. If you haven't yet tried these sources, prepare to be amazed! *The Real Book* also contains copyright and publisher information for each tune, information that is extremely valuable for the arranger.

Transcriptions
Transcriptions are a very profitable tool. By transcribing you will gain insight on both melody and the changes, and will improve your ears at the same time. You will develop melodic and harmonic arranging language that will find its way back into your writing. Be careful, though, to stay within the permissible copyright boundaries. (See Appendix A.)

Song Forms and Layout

Song forms are the structures on which most music is built. *Basics in Jazz Arranging* will focus primarily on the two most common forms (ABAB and AABA), as well as their influence on the process of arranging. Stay with these forms at first. They are the most easily understood, thus freeing more of your mental energy for creative thought.

ABAB Song Form

The **ABAB song form** consists of two eight-bar sections (A and B) that repeat to complete the 32-bar song form. As music passes from A into B, the emotional level should rise. This is referred to as the **contour** and will first occur within the tune itself. The contour is represented here by the dotted line.

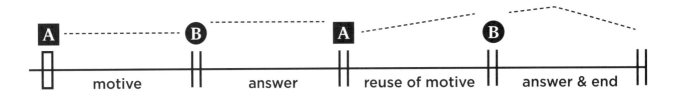

The change in contour usually is caused within the tune itself, since well-written A-B sections have a question-answer relationship. When this effect is not present, the arranger makes up for it with a change in groove or scoring.

In "Turning One" below, the two B sections are similar but not the same. This is normal for ABAB tunes heard in jazz settings. (See Chapter Four for more information.) Check out the sound of this tune and its bossa nova groove on the listening CD, Track 4. Its simplicity is intentional: players and listeners have room to extend their imagination. More great jazz tunes with the ABAB form are available online and on CD as listed on page 6.

Example: "Turning One #1"

AABA Song Form

The **AABA song form** operates differently. The two A sections tend to be mostly the same, except for their cadences. The similarity calls for a contrasting B section, called the **bridge**. The contrast here is due to a change in rhythm, range, or sometimes in underlying rhythmic style, and is sometimes great enough that we refer to it no longer as contrast, but as a **departure**. This terminology separates the levels in contrast between the ABAB and AABA song.

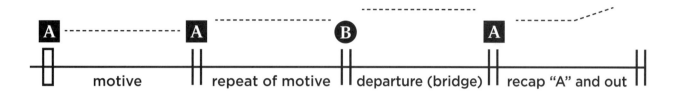

As in the ABAB form, the change in contour usually is caused within the tune itself, since well-written bridges have a noticeable difference to the A sections. Also, as in arranging an ABAB song, when the change in contour is not there, the arranger makes up for it with a change in groove or scoring. In "Turning Two," the bridge (B) has longer note values and is more linear. (See Chapter Four for more information.)

Example: "Turning Two"

"Turning Two" is also on the listening CD, Track 12. As in the case of "Turning One," the simplicity in "Turning Two" is intentional. More standard tunes with AABA form include such greats as "Lullaby of Birdland" (George Weiss/George Shearing), "My Funny Valentine" (Richard Rodgers/Lorenz Hart), and "Skylark" (Johnny Mercer, Hoagy Carmichael). And again, the standard jazz repertoire listed by song form is found at the end of this chapter. (See Chapter Four for an expanded version of "Turning Two.")

Layout

Lastly, the arrangement itself will take on a form of its own, apart from the tune itself. Generally, for most small group charts where soloing is an objective, the **outer form** will be **A-B-A**. (A for the intro and head, B for soloing, then returning to A for the recap and out.) On the recap A, many times the entire head will not be repeated. The determining factor is clocktime, as well as whether the nature of the tune itself has enough interest level to compete with great soloing in the middle section. This is a judgment usually made by the arranger, and many times discussed by the performing group. The wise arranger remains flexible.

Starting to Work

Good arrangements are always the product of good preparation. Suggestions:

- Prepare your ears. Temporarily limit your listening to jazz recordings that feature the style in which you have chosen to write. Prepare your ears also by transcribing some of the sounds you hear that are most attractive to your ears. (See the discography on page 38.)

- Provide yourself with a lead sheet that is free of built-in errors. Remember that the Hal Leonard and Sher Real Books are reliable in this sense. Avoid using only older sheet music.

- Begin to "work the tune" at the piano. See "Arranger's Piano" (below) and "Working the Tune" (page 5).

- Begin sketching only when you have ideas that feel good to your ear. Check out "Arranging Strategies" in Appendix A. Also, see Chapter Seven for perspectives on the sketching process itself.

Arranger's Piano

"Arranger's Piano" involves simple voicings:

- Three up, one down on most chords. (Examples A, B, and C below)
- Three up, two down on spread m9 and 13th chords. (Examples D and E)
- Four up, one down when needed. (Example F)

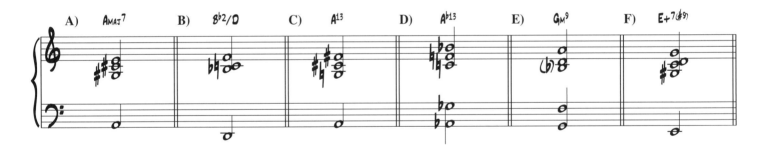

Exercise: Spend 15 minutes three or four times a week.

- Work with tunes you've learned on your primary instrument.
- Play the root-position voicings shown above on the chord changes of the tune of your choice.
- Use *rubato* generously. There is no need for speed at this point.
- Avoid thick voicings in the left hand.
- Do not permit playing the melody to compromise your chord voicings.
- Add chords and inner movement to the changes. Explore your harmonic ear.

Working the Tune

Working the tune is a process of experimentation, involving the piano. Many ideas that wouldn't occur otherwise are discovered via the following guidelines. Especially for non-keyboard musicians, this routine is invaluable for discovering sounds that you might not know were there. On the abbreviated copy of "Turning Two" (below), try the following:

- Play "Turning Two," in or out of tempo. If you are not a keyboardist, play just the chords.

- Play the cadences. What happens when you substitute other cadences?

- "Turning Two" chord changes move over an E bass. Can you re-harmonize the first four bars?

- Go to Appendix E on page 119. If "Turning Two" — written to completion and located on the Listening CD, Track 12 — causes your ear to imagine other musical thoughts, sketch them now.

Example: "Turning Two" – AABA

- See **Chapter Two** for perspectives on jazz melody and melodic development.
- See **Chapter Three** for examples of jazz harmony and how it works.
- See **Chapter Four** for ideas on composing your own material.

Standard Tunes, Listed by Their Song Form

Tunes on this list have proven themselves over the course of time. Great recordings are available for each of them, for research and listening purposes. (Check your favorite online retailer.) It is easy to identify artists who have recorded these tunes. On the Internet, research by title from either ASCAP (www.ascap.com/ace) or BMI (www.bmi.com). Lead sheet versions are available in many popular *Real Book* editions as well.

AABA Song Form

Medium or Up Tunes
A Night in Tunisia
Afternoon in Paris
All The Things You Are (hybrid)
Autumn Leaves
Bernie's Tune
In Walked Bud
In Your Own Sweet Way
Lullaby of Birdland
Moten's Swing
Nardis
Robbin's Nest
Satin Doll
Stella by Starlight (hybrid)
Stompin' at the Savoy
Take the "A" Train
We'll Be Together Again
Well, You Needn't
What Is Thing Thing Called Love?

Ballads
Darn That Dream
I Got It Bad (An' That Ain't Good)
Ill Wind
In a Sentimental Mood
My Funny Valentine
What's New?

Latins
I Love You
The Girl from Ipanema
Night and Day
This Masquerade
Wave

ABAB Song Form

Medium or Up Tunes
All of You
Beautiful Love
But Not for Me
Days of Wine and Roses
Dearly Beloved
Easy To Love
Four
Gone With the Wind
Green Dolphin Street
I Could Write a Book
I Should Care
I Thought About You
In a Mellow Tone
Just Friends
Love Is Here to Stay
My Romance
There Will Never Be Another You

Ballads
Dolphin Dance
Here's That Rainy Day
Spring Is Here
The Party's Over
The Very Thought of You
Yesterdays

Latins
Black Orpheus
How Insensitive
Out of This World
The Shadow of Your Smile
Triste

CHAPTER TWO
JAZZ MELODY

Melody is normally the ingredient most responsible for the success of a tune and its arrangement. This is not to discount harmony, rhythm, and orchestration, but successful arranging is dependent upon one's management of melody and the way it breathes within whatever style is present. For this reason, the arranger's ears become increasingly analytical as we hear successful music being performed, remembering what really worked, as well as scoping the scores of great music, even in differing styles.

Simple Analysis

Analysis in this chapter is very basic, limited to three important functions: **structure**, **implied harmony**, and **character**. Cadences, both melodic and harmonic, are an important part of the structure. All of these functions work to hold the music together. Therefore, they are vital tools for the arranger while in the beginning stages of a new chart.

Structure

Structure describes the way music is held together. Most music consists of **phrases** and **periods**, ending in (or held together by) **cadences**. When these structural elements are handled well, performer and audience are pleased — their interest continues. When the elements are predictable, the listener begins to lose interest, and the performer hopes that the paycheck will make up for it.

The **phrase** is the shortest section of music ending in a cadence. The most common phrase length is four bars. Four-bar phrases may combine into eight-bar sections that are called **periods**. A phrase will normally end with a longer note or longer rest before the music proceeds. This is the **cadence**, a most important member, since this is where the melody breathes.

In the example below, the first phrase (bars 1–3) is sequenced in the second phrase (bars 4–7). The third phrase (bars 4–11) starts the B section, while the fourth phrase (bars 12–15) wraps it up. The score for "Upstairs" is in Appendix E. The recording is on CD Track 1.

Example: "Upstairs"

Periods are the primary building blocks for a standard length tune of 32 bars. In terms of musical form, these periods are identified by letter names. Most older and more basic jazz tunes and standards have the form of ABAB or AABA, as mentioned in Chapter One. While a formal and theoretical background does not write the music for us, without these concepts well in hand, we lose much valuable time in endless experimentation.

These letters describe the way that "Upstairs" is constructed. While the form is neither ABAB nor AABA, "Upstairs" shows characteristics of both in an interesting hybrid form. The B section operates like a B from ABAB, and C is like the bridge (or B section) from an AABA form. This is very important.

Cadences

Cadences are the combination of notes, chords, and rests that slow the forward movement of music, causing a sense of pause. Some cadences are shorter, some longer, some obvious and others less so. The importance of this is that predictable music will be heard differently than unpredictable music. For example, we sometimes choose to delay or subvert the cadence function, to hold the listener's attention. This can be quite effective when handled tastefully. Recognizing interesting and effective cadences greatly increases the value of our listening.

Cadences built from harmonic and melodic elements are the most basic. Chapter Two focuses only upon these. Other types of cadences are discussed later.

The **melodic cadence** is a break in the forward movement of a melody line. This is usually caused by a longer note that occurs at the end of a phrase (bar 3 below) or period, or by a note followed by rests (bar 7).

Example: "Upstairs"

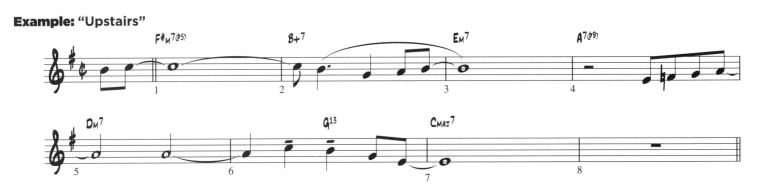

Harmonic cadences are chord progressions that interrupt forward movement in music, thus letting the music breathe. They generally occur at the end of phrases or sections. Both types of cadences — melodic and harmonic — play a vital role in the success of music that we write. Keeping track of how these cadences work together is an important part of good arranging.

Harmonic cadences are **half** or **full**, depending upon where they occur. They support the way a melodic line is constructed, an important consideration for the writer.

The half cadence is usually a ii–V or IV–V occurring at the end of a phrase. But virtually any progression that ends in a V where a cadence is expected will operate like the half cadence. Melodic activity above the half cadence usually slows down as well.

Example: "Upstairs"

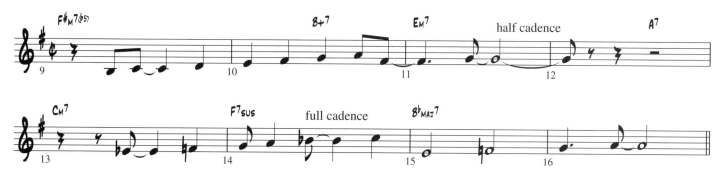

The **deceptive cadence** (V–VI where V–I is expected) is valuable to signal a "turnaround." In the following example, the first four bars end with V–VI, a deceptive cadence that calls for a turnaround extension. The four-bar extension cadences not with V–I, but with IV–I, the **modal cadence**, which is valuable for its bluesy sound.

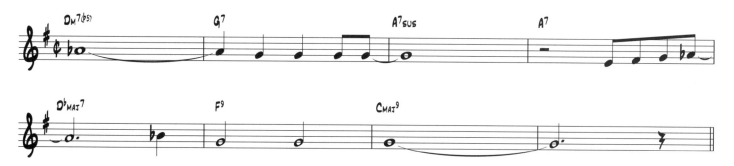

The **full cadence** is normally a V–I progression occurring at the end of a section, as shown below.

Virtually any progression ending with what feels like a tonic chord will operate like a full cadence, providing the melody line slows as well. Be aware, however, that too many full cadences will destroy otherwise good music, because of too many stops in too short a period of time.

"Upstairs" appears on the next two pages as an expanded lead sheet with voiced changes. Play this slowly at the piano and listen to the effect caused by the various cadences. Note that chords agree with the chord symbols, and are constructed according to "Arranger's Piano." (See page 4.) If your keyboard ability is limited, play in a slower tempo, or even totally out of tempo.

UPSTAIRS

By Paris Rutherford

Exercise #1: Choose a recording that you admire and analyze the cadences of the first full minute of the recording. Draw a schematic for this. Include tempo, clock time, types of cadences, and the chords involved. This is very profitable.

Example: "Upstairs" – ♩ = 152

	ii–V	passing	II – V	full cadence	
					14 seconds
Bars	1 2 3	4 5	6	7 8	

Exercise #2: Now transcribe the melody line. By creating the schematic first, your transcription will be even more beneficial to you.

Implied Harmony

Whenever a melody moves, the melody itself suggests a sense of harmony of its own. We refer to this as **implied harmony**. (Harmony expressed by composer's chord changes may or may not be the same as harmony implied by the melody itself.) It is usually different in jazz — when implied harmony and the chord changes are very similar, the effect is that heard more commonly in pop music. When different, you have music with a more engaging level of interest. First the composer, then the arranger, controls these subtleties.

In the next example, C major is implied in the first four bars of "Upstairs," where the melody comes from the upper half of the C major scale. An Am7 chord is implied in the second phrase, which outlines an Am7 chord.

Now let's compare the implied harmony above to the composer's chord changes below. Though they differ, they are compatible to each other. The arranger adjusts the interest level by moving implied harmony and composer changes closer to or farther away from each other.

Analysis of these harmonic implications enables the arranger to control tension levels and musical style. Some styles and situations require more tension, some less. To review:

- When implied harmony agrees with the written changes, the level of tension is low. The music may be beautiful and pleasing to the ear, but requiring little thought. This does not match our expectations for jazz.
- When implied harmony and the changes differ, the level of tension increases and is measured by how far apart they have moved. Now there is the beginning of an esoteric quality that is common to jazz, but unacceptable in most pop music. (No criticism of pop is intended here; this is just a statement of reality.)

Interestingly, this careful handling of the melody and primary bass line (the changes) is seen in all music, all styles. This is especially true in film music, where both composer and orchestrator carefully raise and lower the level of tension according to the needs of the picture and script. That is two-part music at its best!

Implied harmony is expressed through...

...Stepwise movement beginning on or approaching a strong beat. Identify the scale. The implied harmony for that section of melody will carry the same name. In the example below, the last three eighth notes of bar 2 serve as pickups to the longer downbeat; they come from D♭ major.

...A broken chord (arpeggio). Analysis is made based on any position or inversion of a chord formed by the majority of notes involved. (Note the chord symbols.) Once again, the last three eighth notes of bar 2 constitute a pickup to the longer downbeat: the arpeggiated chord changes the implied harmony from A♭ major to Fm.

The value in analyzing a tune's **implied harmony** is great. If arranging for a young group, we stay close to the implied harmony at first. For a more experienced group, we choose harmonies that are compatible, but not as simplistic as the example above. Note the difference, below:

...Appoggiaturas and **escape notes**. An appoggiatura is a jump/step, while an escape tone (*echappée*) is a step/jump. The outer two notes will suggest a chord or two, reliable as long as the shapes are genuinely non-harmonic. In the example below, there is an appoggiatura in bar 1 and bar 2, and escape notes in bar 4.

Review. When writing in jazz styles, too much agreement between implied harmony and the actual changes can become expensive. As said earlier, the interest level can become too low for the music to feel appropriate to the jazz style. If the chosen tune is a good one, you can use chord substitutes to change the bass line (Chapter Three), thereby changing the harmonic relationship between melody and bass line.

Melodic Character

The melody line moves in a way that is considered either **active** or **static**.

Active describes a melody containing skips and/or sudden changes of register. When only a few horns are involved, an active melody moves best with unisons (and octaves).

Example: "Traveling" – unison horns, unison rhythm

Note, however, that rhythmic complexity alone does not classify melody as active. Leaps or abrupt changes of register, etc., may be present as well.

Static is the opposite of active. Static melody consists of stepwise movement, sustains, and rests. Sudden changes in register are kept to a bare minimum. The use of horn voicings sounds more appropriate on static melody than on active melody. The example below is from the bridge area (letter B) of "Turning Two." (See Appendix E, page 122.) The melody is entirely stepwise, and the horns are scored with a variety of voicing types.

Example: "Turning Two" – three horns, rhythm section

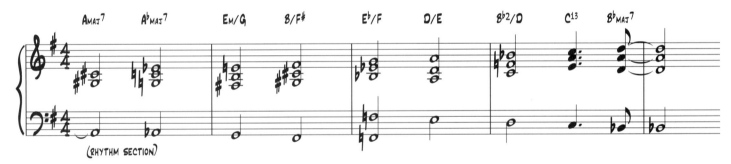

Obviously, analytical terms such as **active** and **static** can be difficult at first for the writer unaccustomed to such analysis. But when they become part of one's musical life on a daily basis, we move from being casual listeners into composer/arrangers that remember more accurately the sounds that we enjoy and respect.

TRAVELING

By Paris Rutherford

"Traveling" can be heard on CD Track 3. Its score is located in Appendix E, page 98. The style is a modern version of the New Orleans Street Beat, and the label "Brookmeyer Bit" refers to a short but marvelous area in a Bob Brookmeyer big band recording where several players improvised aggressively at the same time. We chose "Traveling" to try this out. Enjoy the result!

Adapting the Melody

Adapting the melody is the simplest form of arranging, and involves only four steps.

- Determine the style in which the tune is to be played. (Swing, Latin, straight-eight, etc.)

- Select the best key for the circumstances at hand.

- Make simple adjustments to the rhythm of the melody to conform it to the chosen style. When a tune should swing, sheet music rhythms don't work.

- Notate and print the material accurately for the performers, transposed when transposing instruments are involved. (Use chord symbols found in *The Real Book*.)

When a **simple adaptation** is all that is required, it can be accomplished in a matter of minutes. The melody line may need only to have its rhythms adjusted to fit the jazz style, and would be played only once before soloing begins. When a project calls for more **extensive manipulation**, the arranger should still begin with the first three of the steps above.

Selecting the Best Key

Place the range of the tune (distance from highest to lowest notes) within the average playing range of your top or lead horn. (For average playing ranges, see page 74–76.)

Example: "Turning Two" – last five bars

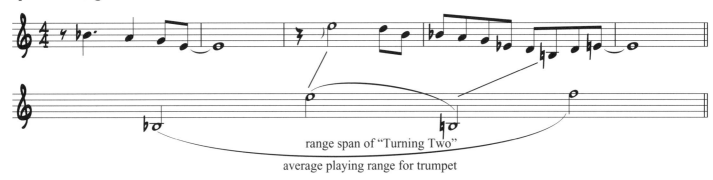

If there's room, locate the span of the tune closer to the bottom of the average playing range (APR) if the lead is a higher instrument (trumpet, alto sax, etc.), especially if the tempo is to be slow. Locate the span closer to the top of the APR if the lead is a lower instrument (trombone, tenor sax, etc.) or if the tempo is to be faster.

Fine tuning the **selection of best key** is important. Brass and woodwind players are most experienced playing in keys ranging from two sharps to five flats (concert). Therefore, when the choice of concert key is between, say, B♭ major and B major, your players will probably be at their best more quickly in B♭ major.

Adjusting the Rhythm of the Melody

When writing in a swing style, analyze the melody for rhythmic placement. This means that if too many strong notes fall on the beat, the music cannot swing properly. Syncopate a few to relieve this problem.

- **Locate the phrase that needs to be adjusted.** Syncopate first at the end, then earlier as needed. Sing the line you have adjusted! If you can sing it, whatever your sound, the instrumentalists can play it. If your rhythms don't feel easy as you sing the line, they won't play out any better!

Example: "Turning Two" – Letter C

When a tune with lyrics is being sung and the style is "in two," these rhythms are okay.

When the tune is being played by a small group, the melody is adjusted to swing.

For a faster tempo, more space is needed to balance horns and rhythm.

- **Adjust the rhythms so that there is a good flow.** Don't be clever with syncopations; rather, listen to good models as you arrange. Remember always that as you are writing melody lines for the horns, there is also a rhythm section. Your melody lines need to breathe!
- When you have finished adjusting the melody, and before having the chart performed, **check for unwanted symmetry in your melody line.** Look first at the phrases. If you see the same rhythms at beginning or end, make a slight change. See bars 1 and 3 above.

Adding to the Melody

In most jazz arrangements, the melody undergoes some development to fit the style or the personality of the performing group. At times, you may decide to add a few notes to the melody line. This can be a positive step, as long as the nature of the tune itself is not compromised.

When adding notes, first identify the **keynotes** of your melody. The keynotes are those primary notes around which a melody is built. They are easy to find, and must be protected. "Upstairs" is composed from the primary notes shown in the following example. Underneath are the keynotes we protect.

Example: "Upstairs"

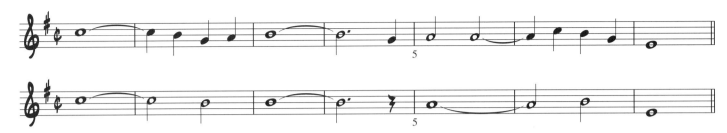

Adding notes to a melody will not change the nature of the tune if the additions fall into one of two categories: non-harmonic shapes (see below) or chord tones from the changes themselves. In bar 2, the melody was adjusted to swing. Notes were added for style in bar 4, and the added notes in bar 6 are non-harmonic and obey the changes.

The **non-harmonic shapes** are shown here. They are identical to those in classical theory.

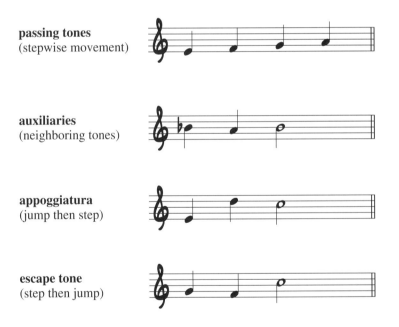

"Upstairs" was arranged for and recorded by trumpet, tenor sax, and four rhythm. Note several adjustments of the melody.

- The melodic figure in bar 2 is inverted in bar 6.
- In bar 13, a note was omitted from the sequence.
- In bar 24, note the added space in the first half of the measure.

The recording of "Upstairs" is on Track 1 of the CD. The full score is located in Appendix E.

UPSTAIRS

By Paris Rutherford

CHAPTER THREE
JAZZ HARMONY

Jazz lives in a world all its own. In the areas of harmony and melody, jazz is written and performed with a higher level of harmonic color than most other popular styles. In addition, the improvisation so prevalent in jazz helps to raise the harmonic color.

Chapter Three explores jazz harmony from the standpoint of the writer. Arranging and improvising coexist within the same basic harmonic system. When improvising, though, the musician approaches harmony differently than when composing and arranging. The primary difference is time frame. Improvisation is spontaneous — an arrangement lasts forever.

To understand the logic of jazz harmony we begin with the I and V7 chords. Refer to the examples below.

- In many other styles, the tonic in a major key is a major triad. **(Example A)**
- In jazz, though, tonic is usually an extended chord: maj7, maj9, etc. **(Example B)**
- Stretched to two hands, the root of this Cmaj7 chord is located in the bass clef. (See **Example C** below and "Arrangers Piano" on page 4.)
- In many styles, the dominant 7th chord is a normal idiomatic sound. **(Example D)**
- In jazz, the dominant 7th chord becomes idiomatic only when extended or altered. **(Example E)**
- And, when actually played, the root of any of these chords is relocated to the low register. (In jazz keyboard fundamentals, comping figures in the left hand play only the root of the chord in the bass range.) **(Example F)**

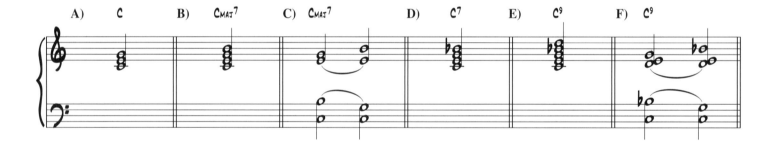

The importance of these guidelines increases greatly as a jazz arrangement grows in size.

Two-Part Structures

Jazz music travels in **a two-part structure** consisting of **melody** (part one) and **fundamental bass** (part two). Part one includes everything associated with the melody line, whether single instruments or grouped voicings. Part two includes everything associated with the bass line: the chord changes (whoever plays them), background sounds, and the rest.

Example: "Porch Time"

Fundamental Bass

Why the label **fundamental bass**? Because in analyzing chord changes for chord substitution or reharmonization, we are less interested in the notes actually played in the bass line and more interested in the basis (or fundamental) of the chord change itself.

The fundamental bass, then, represents the primary bottom notes in a set of chord changes. One note is sustained for each chord, no matter how long or short its duration. Sometimes the fundamental bass is the root of the chord, sometimes not — but it always represents the pitch at the root of the changes. (Fundamental bass is an analytical tool, not intended for performance.)

Intervals between fundamental bass and melody help to define style. Intervals of 2nds, 9ths, 7ths, etc. are more jazz-worthy than intervals of unison, octaves, and 5ths. When octaves and 5ths are necessary for the tune itself, the arranger can follow them with different chords that agree with the melody. Originally, Letter B of "Porch Time" suggested the following:

Example: "Porch Time"

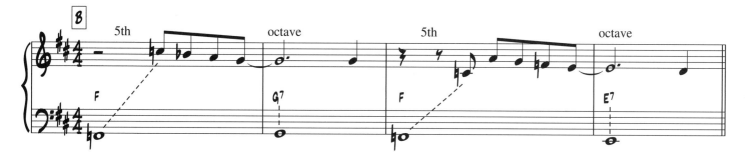

Problem. Between the melody and the fundamental bass, the 5ths (bars 1 and 3, F–C) and octaves (bar 2, Gs; bar 4, Es) are not jazz sounds. Play the example above and hear the effect.

Solution. In the example below, change-bass (bar 2) and compatible chords (bars 3–4) improve the sound.

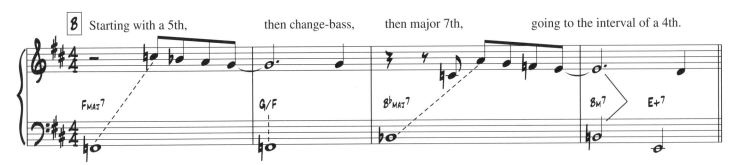

The truth is, we cannot substitute all the ailing two-part intervals without the risk of compromising the tune or its style. This becomes a judgment call. Extensive listening enables us to make the best choices under these varying circumstances.

Chord Substitutions

Why substitute chords? To change the way the bass line reacts with melody, to convert some pop tunes to a jazz feel, or sometimes just to please the ear of the arranger!

Common substitutes (primary and secondary) are built over bass notes a 3rd or 5th above or below the original bass note.

- The **primary substitute** is based a 3rd away from the original chord: they share two notes in common.
- With only one note in common with the original chord, the **secondary substitute** is weaker, but is okay nonetheless. Its bass is located a 5th up or down.

Major chords. Locate a new bass note (see above) and select the right chord. The number of common tones will influence the music's energy level.

Minor chords. Locate a new bass note (see above). Since minor chords are more common to jazz, these substitutes are extremely valuable to the arranger.

Dominant Chords. Locate the new bass note a tritone (A4 or d5) away and build a new chord. A dominant or diminished chord will work equally well, since both will contain the same tritone as the original.

Review. The **chord substitute** is so named because of its ability to do the job of another chord whose fundamental bass needs to be changed. The success of such substitution relies on notes in common between the two harmonic areas.

Putting this to work. In "Upstairs," harmonies in bars 18–25 were adjusted several times. The example below demonstrates this process. The first harmonization had the chords shown. They were okay, but to our ears there were too many A minor sounds (bars 18, 19, 22, 23) and one more A fundamental than the tune needed.

Example: "Upstairs"

Harmonies were changed: in bar 18, Am7 was subbed to F#m7♭5. Then, a descending bass line to add interest (bars 20–21 and 21–23) and the removal of three 5th/octave relationships between fundamental bass and primary melody. As usual, the final harmonization of "Upstairs" was our third attempt.

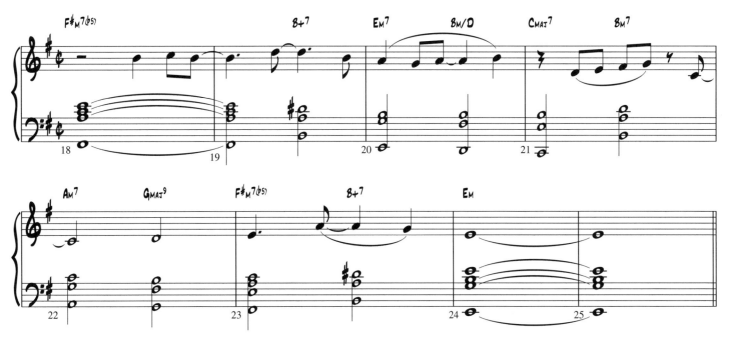

Adding Chords to the Changes

Sometimes even a great set of chord changes needs additional harmonic movement. This could be due to a change in tempo or a change in the musical style. When the need is present, chords may be added without changing the basic harmonic message. Only the flow and number of chords used will change.

This process is called **add-chord**. Selection of chords and their shape is made on the basis of non-harmonic shapes added to the fundamental bass. (Stepwise bass was shown on page 23.) Add-chord is sensitive to tempo and chordal movement. That is, the speed with which the melody moves will determine the number of **add-chords** that may be used.

"Upstairs" (basic) is harmonized with simple but playable changes, written here for demonstration purposes. On the demonstration recording, those changes were played.

Example: "Upstairs" – generic changes

At the top of page 25, "Upstairs" (medium tempo) has additional harmony by way of the **add-chord** process. In the second full bar, the F9 chord is added via **appoggiatura** (jump-step) and the F9–Em7–Am7 progression by way of **escape tone**. Bars 4 and 5 have chords added by stepwise bass.

Example: "Upstairs" – add-chord

The **add-chord** device is utilized even more in the next example, which is at a slow tempo. Slower tempo permits some extreme additions to the chord changes.

- The fundamental bass in bar 2 now has the shape of an **escape tone**.
- The fundamental bass in bars 4–6 follows a jazz version of the Lydian scale.

Example: "Upstairs" – slow tempo

Music from many of the most lengendary jazz composer/arrangers contains changes of this nature, from Byers to Brookmeyer.

Harmonic content in any arrangement can and should be tailored to the need. When one begins to use the devices found in this chapter (substitutes, change bass, alterations, and add chord), the result is usually excessive at first. For this very reason, first attempts at using these devices should be recorded in the notation program you use, and permitted to rest for a day or two while your ears become accustomed to the new sounds. This is an exciting and productive process, to say the least.

Application. Play through the three sets of chord changes for "Upstairs" (generic, add-chord, and slow tempo) to hear the difference. All three honor the melody, but in different settings.

In addition, the use of "Arranger's Piano" (page 4) at any speed is a very good learning tool. To experiment with "coloring the changes," try putting chords between the treble and bass notes in the following exercise. Also, in or out of tempo, avoid using the same type of chord too many times. Experiment. It's fun!

CHAPTER FOUR
BASIC JAZZ COMPOSITION

Once their career is underway, most jazz performers and educators write at least some of their own original material. There are three reasons:

- Playing some of your own music can be more satisfying than being restricted to performing only the music of others.
- As your music becomes available to the performing community (recordings, performances, etc.) there are royalties.
- Developing as a composer, even just of tunes, will boost your musicianship.

When to start? Right now! Musicians who wait too long to begin composing usually find themselves hampered. Why is this? Because their performing and/or teaching careers are too well-established for them to expose their earliest attempts at composing to the ever-present community of eager critics.

Chapter Four has one goal: to provide guidelines that, when followed, will promote quick and enjoyable success in writing tune material. Everyone will interpret these guidelines differently. This is okay, as long as you allow the guidelines to influence you. Don't discard them when the going gets rough, which is the very time these guidelines have proven themselves most valuable.

In the Beginning

When beginning to compose an original tune, follow this routine until you no longer need it.

First: Begin by listening to recordings with the harmonic style in which you're preparing to write. Play these sounds at the piano as well (slowly), and memorize their positions on the keyboard. This is the best way of washing your inner ear, at least for the time being, of sounds that you don't want there while you're composing. This is an important preliminary step for the musician who has a steady gig playing rock 'n' roll, or teaching band or orchestra in the daytime. (Unless, of course, those sounds feature the harmonic palette in which you intend to compose.)

Then: Start with an interesting chord progression or melodic fragment (2–3 bars at most, either way). Develop these according to the guidelines found on the next few pages, so that they begin to occupy reasonable space. Generate some material.

And: Concentrate on the material being generated. Develop it into a sustainable form. (See "The Developers" on the following pages.) Let your harmonic progressions develop from cadence areas, right to left according to the re-harmonizing guidelines in Chapter Two.

The Developers

Developers are the primary tools used in jazz composition to lengthen a short fragment of melody into a coherent phrase, and then to combine phrases into longer sections. By utilizing these devices, the composer is able to stretch a good idea into a memorable and interesting length of melody.

Developers are indispensable. Without the lengthening and answering that come from their use, original music can quickly become busy, too densely filled with good ideas that don't relate to each other compositionally. After a little experience in using these tools, the writer finds that they become rather automatic, their use also second nature.

The most common developers are:

- Repeat
- Sequence
- Answer
- Mirror

Repeat

A **repeat** is just that, the reuse of a figure using most of the same notes and rhythms. The **repeat** need not be verbatim, though, keeping every note and rhythm the same. Minor adjustments work well, too, and provide interest, as in this next example. Compare bars 1 and 3 at the beginning of "Turning Two."

Example: "Turning Two"

Sequence

The **sequence** is a reuse of four to eight bars of melody, transposed up or down, usually by one step. Only the melody sequences, though: the changes will move somewhere else to help the feeling of development.

Example: "The Front" – bars 21–28

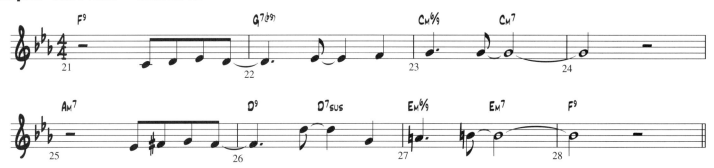

N.B. As the melody sequences (either direction), different chord changes can form a second layer of development, and the sequence itself is protected from being just a transposition of a few bars of music. The direction of a sequence also plays a major role in the development of melody: when music sequences upward (above), the interest level is instantly higher than when it sequences downward.

Answer

The **answer** is a section of melody that completes the thought from a previous phrase or period. The relationship is exactly the same as between the **antecedent** and **consequent** in good sentence construction, bringing a special note to the music that causes the listener to relate with thoughts of personal experience. It is this unspoken bond between writer and performer/audience that makes composing and arranging such fascinating endeavors.

In the example below, the opening four-bar phrase is built on a descending D minor scale. The answering four-bar phrase completes the idea, and is built on the same scale, this time uphill.

Example: "Inner Thoughts"

Then in the next example, phrase one is built on the notes G, B♭, and C. The answer then is built on the descending E♭, D, and C, thereby closing the tonality before going ahead in the tune.

Example: "The Front"

Mirror

Mirror is a reuse of melody in which the intervals are inverted (mirror) or reversed (retrograde). Note that bar 2 and bar 6 have the same intervals, but the intervals are turned upside-down. When not overused, this reuse can be very subtle and effective.

Example: "Upstairs"

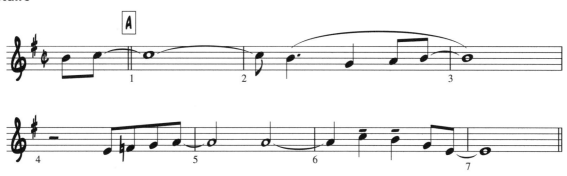

Developers Used in Pairs

The use of multiple **developers** within a section of the melody has a positive effect: the tune fragment or phrase can be developed more creatively without having to introduce new material too soon. This is good for the music as well as for your listeners.

In the example below, notice the following:

- Bar 4 is a sequence of bar 2.
- The last half of bar 9 is a reuse, up a 3rd, of the melody shape in bar 2.
- Bar 11 is a sequence of bar 9.

PORCH TIME

By Paris Rutherford

Vertical Analysis

More than any other single ingredient, the intervallic relationship between melody and bass identifies the style of the music. Pop music and jazz are quite different in this regard. In most pop styles, this two-part relationship must be simple: octaves, 5ths, and sometimes the 3rd. In jazz, these simpler relationships are frequently avoided in favor of more colorful choices.

The two-bar fragment below (bars 1–2) begins to take on some interest when it is repeated in bar 3.

Yet there is no sense of style until harmony is added. Jazz is the goal, so simple intervals (octave, 5th, etc.) survive only when the harmony between top and bottom is rich. In the following example, the 5th in bar 3 relaxes the tension from the use of a tritone in bar 2. This is good.

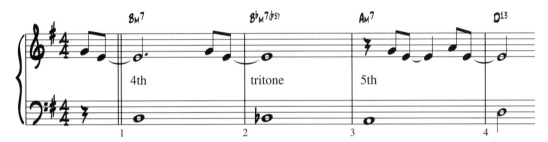

In the example that follows, the first eight bars have a construction of two bars, two bars, four bars, or 2–2–4. When present, this formula tells the composer that the music is free to repeat now. The tune idea has been lengthened and answered, a good formula for the A sections of AABA form.

In this example:

- The opening two-bar motive is repeated, with different changes.
- Bars 5–6 provide an answer for bars 1–4.
- Bars 7–8 allow for some breathing room.

A word about the importance of **answers**: repeating an eight-bar period before there is an answer causes the music to ramble, regardless of how interesting the ideas are. In that case, it would be much better for the eight-bar phrase to be the A of an ABAB form. This is composition at its best!

Song Forms

Composing music to a specific **song form** can be frustrating, thereby slowing the process. Instead, develop your ideas and trust the music to take on form in the process. The formulas mentioned earlier are clues to sort of development that may best fit your music.

We begin to compose without limitations. Then as the music develops and stretches, we impose limitations to control the stretch. Awareness of these simple forms and how they work is most helpful to our reaching the finish line successfully.

Review. The two song forms most common in jazz are **ABAB** and **AABA.** The pages that follow contain guidelines and perspectives on both forms. One melodic thought is developed first in ABAB form ("Turning One") then in AABA form ("Turning Two").

ABAB Form

The **ABAB form** consists of two long stretches of melody, each of which usually begins essentially the same way. In today's jazz, the melodic line needs to feature some interesting variations earlier than it would have a decade ago. This variation should not be so pronounced, though, that it feels like new ideas.

- The first eight bars should end convincingly, but setting up a need to be answered.
- The second eight bars will answer the first eight, finishing the thought. This is now A–B.
- The second 16 bars (A–B, beginning with bar 17) seems to repeat the first. To keep the interest at an appropriate high, different chord changes are used. This is not difficult!
- The 16-bar format is not cast in bronze. Primary sections in ABAB may be shorter or longer by a couple of bars. When you decide to follow this train of thought, look for successful models for help. Don't reinvent the wheel.
- When the music is medium tempo, and extremely rich in its message, you may stop after one time through A–B. Whether to repeat or not is subjective, and should be the subject of some solid research.

Helpful hint. Avoid becoming married to the sound of anything you have composed until you sleep on it and see how much survives. "Turning One #2" (page 33) underwent two complete rewrites, then another three partial rewrites, before reaching the shape it is in now. Five overnight sleep cycles were involved. This is very important to the compositional process.

The recording of "Turning One #2" is on CD Track 9. As you listen, remember that "Turning One #1" was the very careful beginning to harmonizing the tune. Number 2 followed and is the surviving member of the team. The decision was made to finish the first approach before pursuing different harmonies for the tune itself. This is a worthwhile way to maximize the efficiency of your work.

TURNING ONE #2 (ABAB)

By Paris Rutherford

The AABA Form

The **AABA form** consists of two shorter, repeating sections, then a bridge. This bridge should contrast the A sections more seriously than in the second eight of ABAB. For this reason, we describe a bridge with the word **departure**, not just **contrast**.

- The first two sections should begin in the same way, but develop somewhat differently.
- The first eight bars must contain some answering material; otherwise, it can't repeat.
- Since two answered sections lead to the bridge, the bridge must go somewhere else,
- If the music feels totally complete by the end of the bridge, and there is no lyric, you may extend its ending and stop there. **New form: AAB.**
- The level of contrast appropriate for a bridge in AABA would be overkill in ABAB.

You should proceed with the development of your composition, first using the developers, then the harmonic and interval ideas mentioned earlier, and only then applying the perspectives found on this page.

As you put all these things to use, remember that your first efforts must feel good to you. Use the rules only as they help you to succeed. When you refine your first compositional efforts, rules and guidelines are there to assist you in making listenable sense out of the music you have written. The most important development that will occur in your original music will come about automatically overnight, as you sleep on honest hard work. The next day you will refine your music, discarding some of what you wrote earlier, even some portions that felt wonderful the day before. This is typical, so don't sweat it! Never permit your creative brain to become discouraged, because everything worthwhile takes time to develop.

In "Turning Two," note that the melody starts with the formula of 2–2–4: a two-bar theme (bars 1–2), two bars repeated (bars 3–4), then answered with a four-bar phrase (bars 5–8). This developmental formula of 2–2–4 may also be turned around to become 4–2–2 when the ideas seem to work better that way.

TURNING TWO (AABA)

By Paris Rutherford

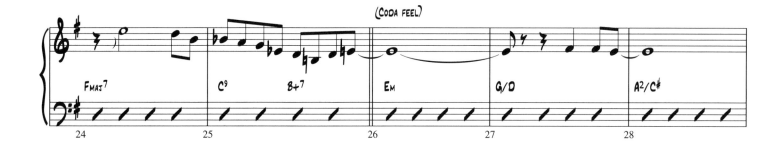

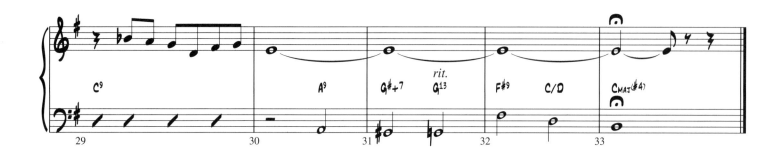

The Blues

The **blues** is essentially a 12-bar form, I–IV–V and repeat. Many liberties have been taken with this truly American song form, but the blues remains nevertheless a happy and swinging act. Jazz greats have delved into the blues in a minor key format, which is also swinging.

For the present, though, we are staying with the B♭ blues, in its most explainable format, the major key. Several things to consider:

- Melody lines in the blues should be harmonically interesting but in agreement with the changes, which (even with additives) will be the traditional I–IV–V, four bars in each stretch. At least, this is the most sensible place to start.

- In the recorded example on CD Track 15 ("The Blues"), there are many D♭s (bars 3, 4, 5, 9, 11), as well as other notes flatted according to the blues scale. This is part of the blues tradition, and fun for people to play. Note, though, that these appear in the moving lines, and not in the B♭ structural melody. This formula works. Try it!

- Since the blues is a short form, the 12-bar **head** is almost always repeated. For this reason, the trombone figures are labeled "2X only," thus giving the head of the arrangement a feeling of being longer than just 12 bars. This is a good plan when there are sufficient instruments involved in performing the composition and its arrangement.

You will notice that in the scores and recordings found in Appendix E and on the CD, the solo areas are shorter than usual. This is because the CD is intended for instructional purposes as part of *Basics in Jazz Arranging*. Were this to be a commercially available product, the solo area would be longer with more departures from the normal "everybody swing, please" format.

The blues is a good place to start composing, and players/singers love the positivity involved in performing the blues. Enjoy!

THE BLUES

By Paris Rutherford

Your First Composition

Now it's time for you to put Chapter Four to use. The guidelines below will assist you as you compose.

- Using a tuneful or harmonic idea of your own, explore it according to the concepts on pages 27–30. Use "Arrangers Piano" (page 4). If you are not a keyboard person, do this slowly and treat your ears to the sound of the melody and chords you think you might use.

- When you have determined the best song form for your composition, use large sketch paper and begin sketching the music with only melody and chord symbols, while including verbal descriptions where you have conceptual thoughts but no music yet.

- Remember that on large sketch paper you can write what you begin to hear, placing those ideas wherever on the page you think they might want to be, in or out of context. (You are the only person seeing your music at this time. Experiment!)

While you are working on your music, listen to great recordings in that style. Do not be concerned at this time with writing something that is too similar to one of the recordings you are hearing. Mark that area. You can change or replace at a later time. Permit your creativity to be influenced by the writers and players you enjoy hearing. This is growth.

Discography of Jazz Small Ensembles

Listed here are a few recordings of well-conceived and well-performed jazz compositions, all by smaller ensembles. The list is incomplete, of course. Add album names as you hear music that charges your creativity. All albums listed below are available through online retailers.

Cannonball Adderly	*Cannonball Adderly*
Art Blakey	*Art Blakey & the Jazz Messengers with Thelonius Monk*
Michael Brecker	*Two Blocks from the Edge*
Miles Davis	*Kind of Blue*
Bill Evans	*The Best of Bill Evans*
Bill Evans	*The Complete Village Vanguard Recordings, 1961*
Erroll Garner	*Concert by the Sea*
Dexter Gordon	*Blows Hot and Cool*
Don Grolnick	*Hearts and Numbers* (with Michael Brecker)
Herbie Hancock	*Cantaloupe Island*
Pat Metheny Group	*Speaking of Now*
Oscar Peterson	*Oscar Peterson Plays the Cole Porter Songbook*
Chris Potter	*Gratitude*
Joshua Redman	*Wish*
Wayne Shorter	*Speak No Evil*

CHAPTER FIVE
THE SMALL GROUP HORNS

The generic name **small group** usually refers to a jazz ensemble of four to seven players. In this chapter, we will refer to all wind instruments as "horns," even though some are saxes or woodwinds. Instrumentation usually includes up to four horns and a three- or four-piece rhythm section. When instrumentation consists of two or three horns, brass and reeds should be mixed if possible. When there are four horns, they can be the same type. Toward the end of this chapter, the addition of voice will be discussed.

Small Group Formats

Mixed horns provide more color, depth, and variety in sound than two or more from the same family. When using only two horns, though, the mix may be in terms of family (brass/sax) or in terms of register (higher/lower). In any event, the best mix will be the horns represented in the best players you can find, especially those who bring with them a sense of involvement.

Chapter Five contains information and perspectives most efficiently put to use in the writing of two arrangements. In both of these, the primary focus is of course upon idiomatic and interesting treatment of melody and harmony. But for the understanding of how horns and rhythm relate to each other, the two charts should be scored differently:

- The **first simple arrangement** should be written for two horns and rhythm. Primary emphasis should be on interesting and idiomatic melodic lines for unison horns. They should breathe properly and exhibit the innate characteristics of the instruments used. If you do not play sax or brass, then transcribe the horn lines from a recommended CD to get started. This will be **Chart #1**.

- The **second arrangement** should be written for three or four horns and rhythm. The emphasis will still be on interesting and idiomatic lines, but with more use of voicings in the horns. The addition of voicings changes completely the melodic and harmonic landscape, no longer restricted to unisons. With this in mind, this second arrangement (**Chart #2**) will involve more color. Therefore, it could be written to a slower tempo, and in a supportive style such as bossa nova or another "eight" feel.

Ranges, transpositions, and basic combinations occupy the first pages of this chapter. Then the focus shifts to the voicing of chords, which when in use will add additional weight to the sound of the melodic lines. The descriptive term for this is **harmonic density**. The "density level" is the number of **different pitches** played at the same time, on the same rhythms, by the horns. We'll say more about this later.

Horns in **Chart #1** should be in unison or octaves, except for a few notes at cadences that could be voiced in 2-density. Of the horns typically used in jazz charts, these combinations work well, each with the advantage found in what we refer to as "color unison":

- trumpet and alto sax (in unison)
- trumpet and tenor sax (if written in unison, they sound in octaves) *
- trumpet and trombone (in octaves)
- trombone and tenor sax (written to sound in unison) *
- flugelhorn and baritone sax (written to sound in octaves)
- trombone and baritone sax (written to sound in unison)

  * *Most frequently used*

Chart #2 should involve three or four horns and rhythm section, horns coming from the same list as before. While the horns will be voiced at times, unison/octave writing does not disappear. Horn groupings should be chosen from the list that follows. These combinations are usually those to which we have easiest access, and they are certainly the most common on CDs that serve as models. When this project involves three horns, the most typical combinations are:

- trumpet*, alto sax, trombone
- trumpet*, alto sax, tenor sax
- trumpet*, tenor sax, trombone
- alto sax, tenor sax, trombone

  The flugelhorn is a good replacement for trumpet when the style is subtle — such as bossa nova and ECM — and the ranges can be kept middle to low.

If the project is to include four horns, see page 49 and Appendix E.

Ranges and Transpositions

Instrument Ranges

Basic **ranges** of wind instruments are divided into the areas of low, average, high, and extended. The chart below carries generalizations that should be observed in the first several charts written for small group. When you write outside the average playing range, you take chances that, while exciting in concept, could compromise the success of your project. This suggestion is not meant to restrict one's individual creativity, but is meant to guide one's early writing (in a style) to success. Upper and extended ranges are more commonly used in charts for the large ensemble (a.k.a. the big band). In the exciting area of jazz arranging, successful performance is always our primary objective.

Follow these playing range guidelines when writing for a small-group ensemble. These ranges are shown for the various instruments in the pages that follow:

- **Lower registers.** Seldom used in small-group arrangements.
- **Average playing range.** Almost all of what is played by small-group horns falls within this range.
- **Upper range.** Seldom used in small-group arrangements.
- **Extended range.** Do not write in this range for the small group.

Brass Instruments

Brass instruments commonly found in the small jazz ensemble include the trumpet, flugelhorn, and trombone. Trumpet and flugelhorn are B♭ transposing instruments. Trombone is non-transposing, written and sounding in concert key. Other brass instruments which from time to time may find their way into jazz ensembles are treated in Appendix C.

Saxophones

Saxophone ranges are easier to remember: they're the same when written in their transposed keys.

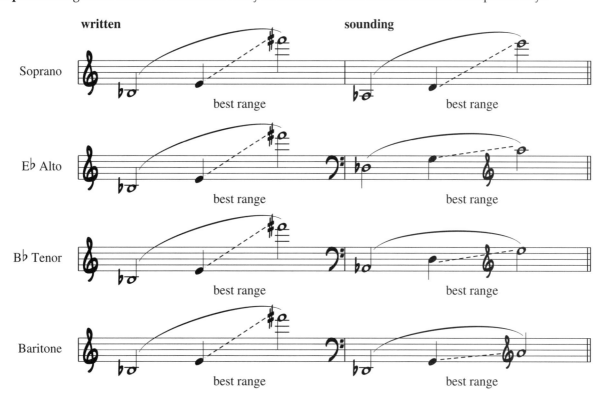

Interpreting the Transpositions

A **transposing instrument** is one whose C sounds a pitch different from that on the piano. The C played on a B♭ trumpet will sound concert B♭, the same as a B♭ on the piano. Throughout this chapter, concert means non-transposed, or concert key.

- **Trumpet and tenor sax are B♭ transposing instruments.** When writing for a B♭ instrument, write everything a whole step higher than it will sound in concert. Also, add two sharps to the concert key signature. For example, when the rhythm section is in C major, trumpet and tenor sax will be in D major.

For trumpet, transpose up one whole step.

For tenor sax, transpose up a whole step plus one octave. The most common transposition error in jazz occurs with tenor tax, so don't forget that extra octave!

The same line, when played by trumpet and tenor sax, will sound in octaves.

- **Alto and baritone saxes are E♭ transposing instruments**. When writing a transposed part for an E♭ instrument, write everything a major 6th higher than concert pitch. Also, add three sharps to their key signature. For example, when the rhythm section is in C major, alto and baritone sax are in A major. When concert key is E♭ major, they are in C major.

For alto sax, transpose up a major 6th from concert pitch.
For baritone sax, transpose up a major 6th plus one octave. Coincidentally, music in concert key written in bass clef, and music transposed to E♭ written in the treble clef, will appear on the same lines and spaces.

The same written line, played by alto and baritone saxes, will sound in octaves.

For additional woodwinds, see Appendix C.

To avoid **overwriting** in your early charts, find two or three recordings of small group sounds that you especially like. Transcribe 16 bars from one in the style and tempo you have in mind. See what the great sounds look like when written down. You will be far ahead of the game this way, when you begin to commit your ideas to paper. Don't be concerned that by transcribing this way you'll end up stealing ideas. There is a certain amount of "sound-alike" in the earlier work of every great writer, any style, any era, since music was first heard. You'll quickly move out of that danger zone.

Harmonic Density

When more than one instrument plays on the same melodic line, or with the same rhythms, the weight of the sound will increase. This effect is measured in terms of **harmonic density**.

The level of density in harmony is equal to the number of different notes found when the instruments on the same line are not in unison or playing in octaves. Density does not describe the number of horns playing on the line, though — 13 horns in a big band could be found playing an aggressive unison line, and the density level is still "one."

Density Levels

Density-1: Harmonic density in **unisons** and **octaves** is at the level of one, no matter the number of horns or other instruments used at the same time.

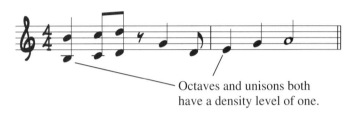

Octaves and unisons both have a density level of one.

Density-2: Two different notes that move together with the same rhythms have a density level of two, regardless of the number of instruments playing. Density-2 will frequently involve a variety of intervals, but only two different notes moving at the same time.

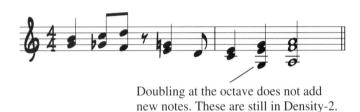

Doubling at the octave does not add new notes. These are still in Density-2.

Density-3: Three notes moving together have a density level of three. Most Density-3 is in close position, and clustering is common.

N.B. Density describes only those notes that move together on a line. When two lines move separately, that is counterpoint, another great writing tool.

When to Write Horns in Density and at What Level

Best choices in using **density** are usually made on the basis of the **character** of the lead line.

- When the leads are **more active** (quicker movement with a wider range), the use of voiced chords is less effective. This calls for a lower density level (unisons and octaves).

Example: "Traveling"

- When the melody line is **less active,** slower and/or with sustains, voiced chords become more effective. This will call for a higher density level, Density-3.

Example: "Traveling"

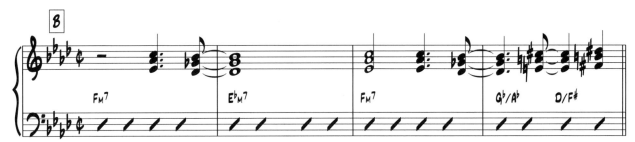

Three Important Considerations

- Both of the above guidelines on **character** will serve you well. Neither, however, is a mandate. Just because a melodic line is active doesn't mean that unisons must be used. When active lines are scored with higher densities, though, the level of aggression becomes noticeably higher. Sometimes this is not the best plan.

- Low, sustained melodies sound good with unisons as well, especially when the chord changes are noticeably colorful. Unisons on melodies with predictable chord changes can be very uninteresting in a jazz setting!

- In instrumental music, frequent changes in density tend to damage the coherency of your music. Here we refer not to number of bars, but "clock time." Listen to some great recordings and see how many seconds go by before the treatment of harmonic density undergoes noticeable change. This is productive listening.

Density of One

Unisons and octaves have a density of one (**Density-1**), regardless of the number of instruments and different octaves that may be involved.

Density-1 is a good choice for lines that have a high level of activity and displacement. See, for example, the excerpt from "Traveling" at the bottom of page 44. Density-1 is also good for normal and slower lines, where higher density can be reserved for special areas, including cadences. Note that, in the following example, the rhythm is bossa nova, so tempo and rhythm section are gentle. The first five bars are unison (Density-1), then move to Density-2 in bar 26 as the melody line goes higher. This allows the style to remain gentle.

Example: "Turning One #1"

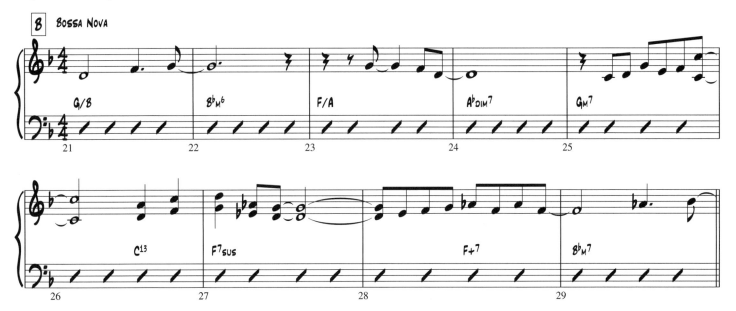

Excellent recordings with Density-1 include "Dolphin Dance" (composed and performed by Herbie Hancock on *Maiden Voyage*) and "Black Orpheus" (composed by Luiz Bonfa, recorded by Wayne Shorter on *Wayning Moments*).

Density of Two

Two-note voicings written with same rhythms have a density level of two (**Density-2**). Density-2 does not refer to the use of octaves, which are still Density-1, or when two lines move against each other with different rhythms, which is counterpoint.

- The most commonly used intervals with Density-2 are 3rds, 4ths, and 5ths. They are best when mixed, and are easily invertible. In the following example, the 5ths shrink to 4ths then to unisons as the melody descends and becomes slower. This mixture of intervals is typical of Density-2 and increases the listener's interest level.

Example: "Porch Time"

- Density-2 can also be used effectively with three horns, with the top and bottom notes in octaves, as seen below in bar 27 and following.

Example: "The Blues"

Great recordings with this density usage include "In Case You Missed It," composed by Herbie Hancock and recorded by Art Blakey (*Album of the Year* CD) and by Bobby Watson (*Live at "Someday" in Tokyo*). Another is "Black Nile," composed and arranged by Wayne Shorter and available on his album *Afro Blue, Volume 2*.

Density of Three

Chord movement with three different notes has a density level of three (**Density-3**). They can appear in both close and open positions, and move effectively at different rates of speed. In small group music, though, Density-3 music should not move at the higher speeds that are more typical of music scored in Density-1.

With Density-3, we first encounter voicings that sound like complete chords. When used in close position, they will usually be in the middle range or higher, and require a bass line to fully agree with the chord symbols.

Density-3 voicings are usually constructed one of three ways, each with its own best use:

- Close-position triads and their inversions
- Close-position chords with the interval of a 2nd
- Quartal triads, built by stacking 4ths

Close-Position Triads and Inversions
Close-position triads and their inversions are quite effective in two usages:

When harmony is simplistic, as in music for young ears, "pop" styles, when melody and the fundamental bass need to be close to each other.

When change-bass harmonies and other unusual sounds need to be scored so that the effect is easy to hear. These should be reinforced by the piano.

N.B. Part of the effectiveness of this example comes from its variety. While the horn line remains triadic and in Density-3, the second example contains change-bass harmonies. In its last measure, the density voicings change shape once to permit better voice-leading.

Close-Position Chords with a Major or Minor 2nd Interval

These are effective in harmonically aggressive and esoteric styles, to involve harmonic extensions and alterations. (Major 2nds are effective both at the top and bottom of a voicing, but minor 2nds are good only at the bottom.) When using this version of Density-3, take care not to stay with any one grouping too long before changing. (This style has been around for quite a while, so its use, while effective, is no longer unique.)

Example: "Traveling" – bridge

Quartal Triads

Additional Density-3 chords with a more open sound involve the 7th interval, which replaces the major or minor 2nd. These voicings are still harmonically rich and used in music where the style is less aggressive. These voicings are called **quartals.**

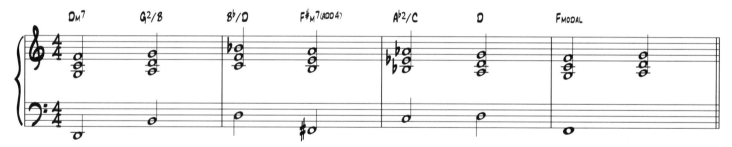

Problem. As popular as these quartal voicings are nowadays in the jazz community, they can be overused. **Solution.** Quartals, tertians, and unisons (octaves) can be combined effectively. The following example comes from the bridge section of "Turning Two." The score is in Appendix E, its recording on CD Track 3.

Example: "Turning Two" – three horns

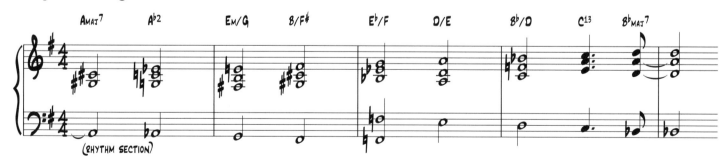

Density of Four

Density-4 involves a rich selection of instruments, and can provide an additional modal quality to the music. While rhythm section players (piano, keyboard, and sometimes guitar) can play four-note chords, we refer in this chapter to density levels used in scoring for non-rhythm section instruments, i.e., the horns.

"Turning Two," originally with two horns and rhythm, is shown here with four horns and rhythm. This is an example of Density-4. The recording of this example is found on CD Track 14. Note the careful voice-leading.

Example: "Turning Two" – bridge (flugelhorn & three saxes)

Before moving on, spend sufficient time at the keyboard with the Chapter Five materials and recordings, playing slowly (or out of tempo) through the examples. Teach your ears to recognize the sounds and the wealth of possibilities available in these varied resources. Successful use of smaller sounds and combinations will greatly enhance the move to large ensemble writing. It's very profitable to internalize these smaller sounds before proceeding onward and upward.

Adding the Human Voice

Basics in Jazz Arranging does not address vocal jazz arranging, per se. But the singer's voice can provide an intriguing and captivating addition to the sounds of a small group.

When added to a unison melody line, a soprano or alto voice can completely change the impression created by the melody itself. Important listening for this effect: the music of Kenny Wheeler ("Sophie," from *Music for Large and Small Ensembles*, ECM label) and "Ela é Carioca," sung by Rosana Eckert (*At the End of the Day* CD). These are good examples of the color available through this mix. (There are no lyrics: the singer uses scat syllables.)

The writer needn't be concerned with the voice being covered up by other sounds in the band. The voice is unison with a horn on the melody or countermelody, and never alone as one of the density elements. Also, in a performance setting, the voice would always be mic'd with a live sound system.

Here are the best ranges for vocals in the jazz and popular idiom:

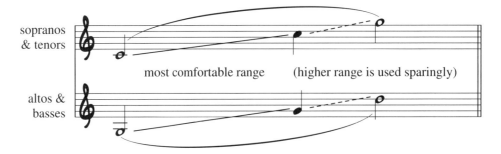

The vocal ranges shown here are for use in selecting the best key for a chart, if not yet written, or for choosing the most appropriate voice type when adding voice (unison) to an existing chart. Shown below is the keyboard part to "The Front." Given to the rhythm section, it contains cues for the unison horn and voice part, an important feature when writing for rhythm and voice. The recording of this is found on CD Track 9. The score is in Appendix E.

Example: "The Front"

Adding Lyrics to a Melody

If the arrangement you are developing is of an original tune, you can also experiment with adding lyrics to the melody. For this experiment to be as advantageous as possible, style and tempo should be similar to the style and tempo of a recording you enjoy hearing over and over.

First, select a topic, such as love, loss, dreaming, etc. Then think of a short phrase that opens the door to that topic in a memorable way. Following these two steps, put your lyrics to eight bars of the melody, changing rhythms and note lengths as needed. After all, this is an experiment, one that could generate wonderful possibilities.

On page 51 are lyrics written to the tune of "The Front." Since "The Front" is an instrumental tune, this new version needed a new title. The name "Together" felt appropriate to the way lyrics developed over time. (The idea of creating lyrics for this tune was born upon hearing voice added to the instrumental version of "The Front.") Scores to both instrumental and vocal versions are found in Appendix E.

While lyric was being created, the first three bars of the melody...

...were adjusted to accept the lyrics.

SOME - TIMES ___ IT SEEMS THAT I DON'T THINK OF YOU. ___

"Together" lyrics
Sometimes it seems that I don't think of you,
That when I wake up I see an empty room.
Well, maybe you think too much of empty rooms.
I believe in you, I cherish you and miss you, my love.
I cherish the thoughts I have of our together times,
Wonderful times, so sublime times.
So when you think I don't think of you, remember,
Remember all the times we had together, together, together.

CHAPTER SIX
THE RHYTHM SECTION

The **jazz rhythm section** must function together as a unit if the music is to be as cohesive as possible. Each player is responsible not only for his/her own playing, but also to contribute to the section feel itself. For this reason, rhythm parts in most arrangements are best kept simple, thereby allowing the players to listen to each other, concentrating simultaneously on the arrangement and to the tightness of their style. Despite the need for simplicity, though, enough specific information must be present so that the rhythm section can deliver what's needed.

Chapter Six will address these needs — keeping the rhythm parts simple, while at the same time providing enough information. Specifics on the different instruments are in Appendix D.

The Basic Rhythm Section

The basic jazz rhythm section consists of **piano**, **bass**, and **drums**. Basic, since these three instruments provide the fundamental needs: the changes, the bass line, and the time. For all rhythm parts, especially the drums, the presence of dynamic markings is very important.

The **bass** plays the line that establishes the chord changes. Whether written or spontaneous, this line fills out the bottom of the two-part structure covered in Chapter Two. Generally, an individual bass part consists of slash notation with chord changes, descriptions in English of what the group is doing, and specific notation when needed. (See Appendix D.)

The **piano** fills out the chord changes, whether from specific music or rhythmic patterns or by comping. The guitar can also serve in this function. When both piano and guitar comp at the same time, one serves as primary, the other secondary. Sensitive players make this decision spontaneously, according to who is soloing.

Drums play time in whatever style is indicated. When the tempo is too slow for the rhythm patterns to be effective without sounding dated, the drummer can fill the rhythm patterns lightly with cymbals and brushes. Either way, most drum music is notated with slashes and instructions, plus rhythmic cues where needed.

Although the basics are covered by piano, bass, and drums, **guitar** is frequently a part of the generic rhythm section, sometimes even replacing the piano. The presence of guitar can enhance a rhythm section in ways too many to cover in this introduction. (See page 86.) **Percussion** may also be involved, especially when the repertoire includes music in Latin styles. (See pages 83–85.)

The Composite Rhythm Part

In simple arrangements, where the melody is played or sung by a single person, or in unison by two or three instruments, the rhythm section usually will play from a **composite rhythm part**. Each player has a copy of this part, which contains the changes, style and tempo, any stop-time music, and occasional instructions for style and soloing — in other words, basic instructions.

The primary value of a composite part is that each of the rhythm players can focus more of their attention on listening to others and playing responsively, than to reading detailed music. Simple charts benefit tremendously from this approach.

The Composite Part with No Melody Line

The composite can be written on a single bass clef line when the tune is extremely familiar, especially if there is only one performer on the melody. (In other words, a gigging chart.) It's understood that specifically notated rhythms or stop time will be played by everyone, unless there are instructions to the contrary.

In this example, everyone plays the rhythmic figures in bars 19–22. In bar 23, the players switch to appropriate comping patterns.

Example: "Upstairs"

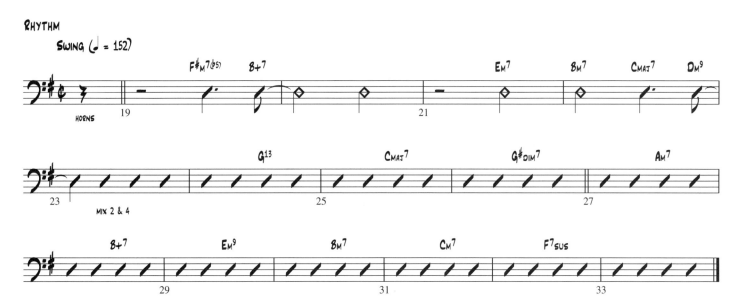

The composite part is also formatted to show the form of the music. Bar numbers and double bar lines are important, as are style and dynamics. Beginning with bar 23, the rhythm part has **slash notation**, which gives each player the freedom to perform according to his/her experience in the present style. Chord symbols are placed above, and cue information below keeps each player alert to special needs.

The Composite Part with Melody Line

More and more in the 21st century, creative rhythm players prefer to see the melody that is being performed. The composite then becomes a two-line part written in grand staff, and is still copied to each rhythm player. (Horn cues are downsized to 75 percent.) When the soloing section comes, this part then reverts to one bass-clef line.

Example: "Upstairs"

Changes, **dynamics**, **style**, and **articulations** are just as important to a rhythm section as to the horn players. Also, since we generally do not write specific notes throughout a drum part, such instructions to the drummer — light fills, four, not busy (and more) — are invaluable to the success of first and second readings. When the arranger prefers that there are no drum fills, the instruction then becomes "no fills." As previously mentioned, **dynamic markings** are helpful to the rhythm section at all times.

When Not to Use a Composite Rhythm Part

- When the need to write specific notes or rhythms would make a composite part too cumbersome and hard to follow. For example, rhythmically aggressive styles. (See Appendix D.)

- When specific notes need to be written for one or more of the players. For example, the arranger may want to write specific lines or voicings for the piano that apply only to that one instrument.

- Major publishers will require individual parts for each member of the rhythm section.

Individual Rhythm Parts

As the number of players increases, or as the rhythmic style requires specific notation, the amount of information needed by the individual players is too great for composite parts. Therefore, the individual rhythm parts become a necessity, and should appear in the score as well.

Slash notation. In all rhythm section parts written in a style where rhythmic interpretation could go several directions, each as correct as the next, you might decide to write a few bars to show your own choice, then give changes alone with *simile* to show that the style should continue. In this next example, specific notation is given to the rhythm section, to agree with the horns.

Example: "Traveling"

TRAVELING

By Paris Rutherford

In the example on page 55, note the *alla breve* time signature, together with 4/4 "slash notation." To see how this is done in computer programming, see Chapter Seven. Also in Chapter Seven are instructions on how to downsize cue notes in the drum part.

Specific notes. Even though pianists need little help with their voicings when they comp or even when specific rhythms are written, you may choose to be specific now and then to show a particular style. In this next example, the pianist is given specific modal voicings that agree with the modality in the horns. When you first decide to take the leap and write out a few piano voicings, follow the guidelines in "Arrangers Piano" (page 4).

More on specific notes. When the texture of the band is complete and harmonically rich, the specific notation for piano is intended both to add more color to the horn harmonies and to prevent the overloading of these rich harmonies by spontaneous additions from the pianist, who would base the note choices solely on chord symbols. This can be dangerous at times.

Lastly, when bass and/or piano are given specific music, the drummer is given specific cues as well. Standard practice is to have specifics for four bars or so, followed by slash notation and changes, with instructions as needed. This example lasts for the full eight bars of the tune's bridge area.

Example: "Turning Two" – bridge

Supporting the Song Form

Musical form is present in all that we write and play. Many times the rhythm section can vary the amount of motion to reinforce the song form of the tune itself. Remember from Chapter One, the AABA form needs a noticeable change to support the presence of the bridge (B).

Sometimes a move from "two-feel" to "four-feel" in the rhythm section is all that is required. In this case, verbal instruction to the rhythm players is all that's needed. "Turning Two" can be played with a "broken two" style for the two A parts, moving to "four" for the bridge, as follows:

AABA – Contour for "Turning Two"

However, varying the motion this way for the ABAB form is less effective. Melodic and harmonic devices account for most of the development within the first chorus of ABAB tunes.

ABAB – Contour for "Turning One #2"

And for the blues, which is a 12-bar form, the rhythm section will establish whatever groove or swing is designated for the head (repeated or not), then change the level of intensity (either up ore down) for the solo area. This is normal, and needs little direction from the arranger.

12-bar blues – Contour for "The Blues"

Review. Write specific music for the small group rhythm section when:
- The style is aggressive and/or Afro-Cuban, and a choice must be made between the various basic rhythm patterns, all of which may be individually acceptable.
- The sounds are modal and you want a specific sound from the exposed section.
- You want the additional color derived from doubling the piano with the horns.

Otherwise, it's best to stay with a generic and composite rhythm part. For specific information on the rhythm section instruments, see Appendix D.

CHAPTER SEVEN
WRITTEN FORMATS & LAYOUTS

Making a Sketch

Sketching is the procedural term that describes the early process of writing music, before going to any level of a final score. During the sketching process, many ideas and concepts are worked out on an experimental basis. Some survive, many do not.

The **sketch**, then, is a material term describing the written product that emanates from the sketching process, differing from a full or partial **score** in several ways:

- The sketch will lack many of the final details one expects to see on a score.

- A sketch can appear in several levels of readability. In its earliest stages, it may make sense only to the writer. The score, though, *must* have a professional appearance.

- The sketch is always written in concert key. The score, when finished, will be transposed. Note: When a score needs to be entered or pointed in concert key, the word CONCERT is placed above bar 1 on page one of the score.

- When the writer is trying new ideas, sketching before going to Finale or Sibelius is by far the best plan. Finale and Sibelius operate only from left to right with no room for experimentation.

It's important to understand, though, that when a writer shows someone his/her sketch, it should be cleaned, with edits and asides removed. A neat appearance is important, even if re-copying is required.

Sketching paper is available in many designs, from two- and three-line formats to full ensemble sketches. Perhaps the easiest design is also the most versatile: that is, a large score page (11x17) minus bar lines. Lines are small. On one page you have enough room to sketch a full minute of music.

The advantage of using large, unlined score pages for your sketching is shown here. You can sketch exactly what you hear (or want to develop), the instant you hear it, and without regard to whether it's sequential or not. (Many times your best work is non-sequential. You make linear sense of it later!)

- The sketch is always in concert key, with horns up and rhythm down. While in sketch mode, it's good to write abbreviated instructions to yourself along with the music. This helps to keep your mind focused on linear ideas, leaving harmonic development and orchestration to come together later when the basic material has become established.

- After spending some good time on searching and sketching, developing new ideas, it is good to let them rest overnight. We then find that the sketching process the next day is more exciting and rewarding than we could imagine. Our brain continues to organize and reorganize our creativity while we sleep, in ways that are almost unimaginable.

- Lastly, whether sketching in two-line or three-line format, it's always good to leave several intervening lines open. It's frustrating to find that your ideas need more space than you had planned. And, when you experience this kind of frustration, some of your better ideas seem to disappear, at least for a while. This is expensive!

When arranging music in any style, for any size group, sketching first and scoring later is the most optimal routine. When music is so uncomplicated that a good sketch carries everything that is needed, even for extracting the individual parts, whether by computer or by hand, we stop there. In this case, the appearance of the sketch must be professional.

Two- and three-line formats are best while sketching. If you are writing for a small ensemble and you cannot fit your ideas into this format, beware. Your music may be too busy.

Example: "The Front"

- Horns in unison are placed in whatever clef is easiest for you. This is a sketch.

- While sketching, it's okay to reverse your format. Just change the clef and go for it.

Example: "Together"

- If you are writing for a vocal solo with rhythm section, the two-line format is good.

However, if the vocal version is with expanded rhythm section or with horns, then a three- or four-line sketch is needed. The reason is simple: when there is a lyric, or even just the sound of the human voice, which carries the thought of lyric even when there is none, we are careful to sketch in a way that protects the range in which the singer is performing.

See Appendix E for the full score of "Together." There is sufficient activity in the rhythm section to support the vocal, so that the addition of horns is unnecessary.

Going to Score

Example: "The Front"

- Transfer your final sketch to the appropriate lines of a small group template, whether in Finale or Sibelius. Whichever program you are using, if you do not yet have your own personal template, it's advisable that you spend the time to make one. When opened then, your template has all the qualities you expect. You then save the template with the title of the music you are preparing to enter. Constructing such a template takes time, but your template will save you a lot of time later on.

- While still in concert key (document or options menu), explode your horn lines down. When first exploded, the unisons (bar 4) will be rests in the tenor/trombone parts. Select that measure on the trumpet line and copy down to the tenor/trombone lines.

- Then, take your score to "transposed." (In some programs, this is accomplished by removing it from "concert key.") **Now is the best time to put in dynamics, expressions, etc. at the right places.** You are now ready to extract your parts. Be very careful when extracting that you use the area in your program that allows you to "manage" the parts, not just "extract."

Extracting the Individual Parts

Individual parts represent *you* to your performers. Good material, appearance, layout, and accuracy will enhance the players' approach even before one note is performed. Once the parts are extracted, check each individually. Though time-consuming, this is worth the effort.

Hand Copying

If individual parts are copied in manuscript, the following suggestions may prove helpful:

- **Paper.** Use a professional weight 10-line paper (minimum 80 lb. weight), which keeps the music from being crowded. Such paper can be purchased from most professional retailers.

- **Pencils.** Use a soft lead pencil for the individual parts (e.g., the Berol Electronic Scorer). Sharpen the pencil frequently to keep stems and bar lines thin.

- **Eraser.** Use the non-abrasive variety, which lifts a pencil's image without damaging the paper's surface. I recommend the Staedtler Mars Plastic Eraser, available from most art supply stores, as well as many university book stores.

- **Rulers.** A triangular and transparent straight-edge ruler will help you keep double bar lines and headings (title, credits, etc.) straight and professional in appearance. If you are using a straight-edge, be sure that it has a beveled edge, so that the pencil's soft leads do not smear.

- **Formatting.** The following guidelines describe individual hand-copied parts that have been strongly appreciated by clients and players for decades, and are therefore highly recommended.
    1. Place instrument name and title on different lines, with the instrument name to the left and the title at the center. The decision of which should be higher and lower is subjective. Imitate the best you see.
    2. Music on page 1 (title page) should **always** begin where line three would be located.
    3. Music on page 2 and subsequent pages should **always** begin at top left.

4. When in 4/4, group four bars to the line, unless due to complex writing the music looks crowded. In this case, let your eye make the judgment call.

5. When in 2/4 or 3/4, you can group more than four bars to the line. Again, let your eyes make the decision.

6. Number each bar at bottom left, to agree with the sketch or score.

7. Page numbers should begin with page 2. On individual parts, place page numbers at bottom left, prededed by tune title.

A Final Checklist

When your music is being read, prior to performance (live or recorded), its appearance will influence the way performers approach the product itself. Realities are not always fair. As you put your music onto computer (Finale, Sibelius, whatever), the program can be made to obey your choice of layout. As you develop and adjust a file and its content to your liking, save it as a template for future use as well. This saves a huge amount of time and mental energy.

Common errors in one's early and simple jazz charts can be avoided by checking our work against this list before the music is seen or played:

- The **sketch** is always written in concert key, with no transpositions anywhere. Where lines are intended to sound in octaves, write one line instead and put "in 8ves" above or below that line. Signal the end of octaves with "unison" or more directly into density writing.

- Material for the **composite rhythm part** appears on the bottom line, in bass clef, and should be identical to that found on the composite part itself, in every respect.

- **Bar numbers** should appear throughout, placed below the staff at the bottom left of each measure. The importance of this increases as your music enters professional and recording scenarios.

- **Clefs** and **key signatures** must appear at the beginning of each page, and should appear at the beginning of each line. Important reminder: a clef sign with no key signature signals that the music is in C major or A minor, whether true or not!

- The **time signature**, though, should appear only once unless there has been a change.

- **Title** and **credits** should be placed so that they appear to occupy a different line space. Instrument name should be at top left.

- **Chord symbols** should be written clearly, and in a style that is easy to read and interpret. Do not be clever with your nomenclature. Rather, be intent with the excellence of your music and its appearance. (See Appendix B for 21st century chord symbols.)

The Appendices that follow contain specific and detailed information that can be very useful when questions arise. And they always do. The author wishes you the best in your pursuit as an arranger and composer in the jazz idiom!

APPENDIX A
ARRANGING STRATEGIES

The Outer Form of the Music

Like the tunes themselves, coherent arrangements will have a recognizable form. Most charts for small jazz ensemble are written with the outer form of ABA.

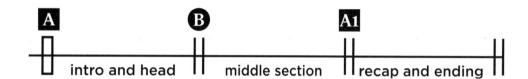

The Intro

The role of an **intro** is to prepare the listener (and player) for what is to come. Your intro will introduce **tempo**, **key center** (probably), and **style**. The chart is now prepared for the **head**.

You can...

- Begin with four to eight bars of rhythm: four for medium tempo, eight for up-tempo. These can be typical iii–vi and ii–V changes, or any standard progressions that will lead the rhythm section into bar 1 of the tune. Piano (or guitar) will improvise through this intro.

- Develop a groove that can continue under the beginning of the head, now using changes that will fit under the beginning of the tune, such as a pedal point.

- Borrow a one- to two-bar fragment from the bridge or from the end of the tune itself that can be developed into a short introductory idea.

You should not...

- Use the beginning of the tune itself, reharmonized or not, for its own intro.

- Write an intro in one groove or style then switch to another for the head. This is confusing.

- Use introductory material that is too long or has too much identifiable interest of its own.

The Head

The **head** is the term that identifies the first time through the tune itself. Be sure that your chart supports and takes advantage of the tune's song form.

- **AABA tunes:** Treat the bridge so that it is a departure from the A sections. Examples:
    1. If writing for two horns, stay unison (or solo) and change the rhythm groove, but not the style.
    2. If writing for three horns, change from voicings to unison for a few bars (or vice versa), or perhaps give the bridge to one of the horns, solo.

If your first two A sections were extremely similar, go somewhere else as you come out of the bridge, at least for the first four bars. This is very important in AABA tunes!

- **ABAB tunes:** Take advantage of the 16-bar length of the AB section to build and develop the feeling of length. If writing for three horns, use unison and octave sounds where the tune has motion. Save density for when the tune climaxes or becomes static. Very important in ABAB tunes: don't write the two AB sections exactly the same way!

Whatever the song form of the tune, take advantage of these traditions:

- Use as many people as you can at all times. Let the playing style and choices in range and register provide ups and downs in the contour. Transparency is commendable, but in your early charts it's good to remember that your best musicians are there to play, not listen.

- If the head will be the only music actually written out, the solo area denoted with the word "solos," be careful where you put chord symbols. Do not put changes over the top of your horn parts in the head. Always write the changes for the solo area, to show the players how you are interpreting the tune. Keep them simple, though.

The Middle Section

The **middle section** develops the ideas from the head. This is done with improvised solos, and perhaps some written material as well. Here are some ideas for you to consider:

- The middle section should not feature the original tune, except perhaps in the background. In this case, use head ideas only if they can be low in register and sustained in nature. It's important that background sounds do not compete with the soloist.

- Your strongest soloist should go first, and rhythm section solos should follow horn solos. If you plan to have a drum solo, let it be the last sounds before the recapitulation. If the first solo is piano or guitar, that sends the signal that s/he is the leader of the group.

- It is unnecessary to feature everyone in the group with an improvised solo. That is for jam-sessions, and therefore inappropriate for a written arrangement.

- If you have strongly reharmonized portions of the head, give the improvisers standard or traditional soloing changes, rather than your reharmonized version.

- If you plan more than one horn solo, and have both piano and guitar in your rhythm section, only one needs to comp at a time. You can suggest different comps behind different solos.

- If you have several solos, find something for the band to do behind last horn solo — written with a lot of space, interesting but non-competitive to the solo. Also, adding a four-bar diminuendo at the end signals a drop in contour for the piano solo. (This is quite optional.)

- Changes of key can be dangerous. Be careful, and follow the models of charts you hear on CDs from the best writers and groups.

Recapitulation and Ending

The movement back to written material is important:

- If the head is extremely diverse (repetitive features not too obvious), reuse the entire head, preceded by a very short drum solo, or the like.

- If the head has obvious repetitive features, or if the tempo is slow, return to the middle:
    If ABAB, D.S. to A and write a Coda to exit the chart.
    If AABA, return to the last A and write a longer Coda to exit — three repeats of something.

- The layout is important. Avoid using D.S. or D.C. if your players must turn pages for the return and then again for the Coda.

- Codas are most effective when they reuse three or four bars of material with different chord changes on the middle repeat, causing an a-b-a effect.

Practical Concerns

Recording Your Chart in a Rehearsal Setting

Always record what you write and perform, even in a reading session. You will hear more from replay after the dust settles than you can remember from the actual playing itself.

Recording tips

- Experiment with microphone placement so that you're able to hear all the parts on replay. Recording quality is less important than balance, especially between piano (guitar) and bass.

- Keep notes on the physical locations of your instruments. Players respect your suggestions on their locations, providing the setup procedure doesn't take too long.

- Open the lid of the piano to face the mic; if an upright, turn the soundboard toward the mic.

- Play only the head once, make comments/corrections, and listen through headphones to a few bars to assess balance. If this takes 15–20 seconds, no one will be impatient. You can then reposition slightly one or two of the performers, but not the drums. Move everyone else!

Copyright Cautions

It is wise to become aware of the provisions within the **U. S. Copyright Law** that address arranging and recording of copyrighted material. The "fair use" of copyrighted material is an issue addressed at the following: www.copyright.gov. This is a wise search for the arranger.

If written permission from the copyright holder is needed or required, we can identify those agencies through www.ascap.com or www.bmi.com. Guidelines on recording can be found within one of the publications on the **music business**. Recommended books are listed in the bibliography found on pages 69–70 .

Timing Your Music

When the clock length of your music is important, the following procedure will prove valuable. Using a computer spreadsheet such as Microsoft Excel, proceed as follows:

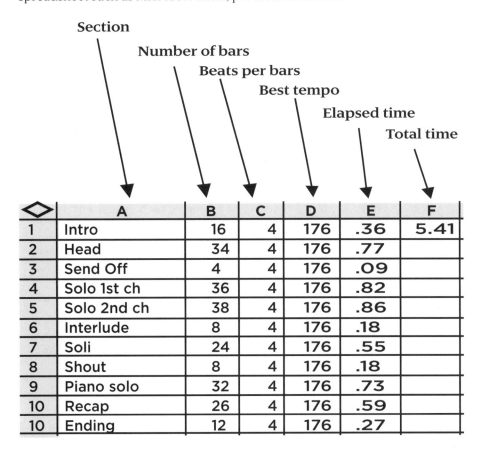

Section → A
Number of bars → B
Beats per bars → C
Best tempo → D
Elapsed time → E
Total time → F

◇	A	B	C	D	E	F
1	Intro	16	4	176	.36	5.41
2	Head	34	4	176	.77	
3	Send Off	4	4	176	.09	
4	Solo 1st ch	36	4	176	.82	
5	Solo 2nd ch	38	4	176	.86	
6	Interlude	8	4	176	.18	
7	Soli	24	4	176	.55	
8	Shout	8	4	176	.18	
9	Piano solo	32	4	176	.73	
10	Recap	26	4	176	.59	
10	Ending	12	4	176	.27	

Formula for the total time begins by touching cells according to the formula above: A is the section of the tune. B is the number of bars in that section. C is the beats per bar in that section. D is the tempo for that section. E is the elapsed time for that section.

Touch B, then the "times" button (*),
  touch C, then the dividing sign (/)
    then D and an equals sign (=)
      This gives you the clock time for that section.

When you have constructed and managed the number of lines that correspond with the length and shape of your chart, then it's time to see the total clock time.

In the space 1F, type this formula: =sum() • then place your cursor in the middle of the () then drag your cursor from top to bottom of column E. The total time will appear in 1F.

The advantage of using this formula: as you make any changes in any of the spaces within the page (such as number or bars, change in time signature, tempo, etc.), cell 1F will immediately respond with the new elapsed time. This can be very helpful!

Bibliography

Jazz Arranging and Composing

Baker, David. *Arranging and Composing for the Small Ensemble: Jazz/r&b/jazz-rock, Revised Edition*. Los Angeles: Alfred Music Publishing, 1988.
  Baker's book is a complete and excellent resource, especially in jazz-related styles.

Delamont, Gordon. *Modern Arranging Technique*. Delevan, NY: Kendor Music, 1965.
  Delamont offers thorough and understandable examination of various aspects in jazz arranging and composing.

Dobbins, Bill. *Jazz Arranging and Composing: A Linear Approach*. Rottenburg, Germany: Advance Music, 1986.
  Dobbins approaches arranging and composing from a linear standpoint. This technique, when acquired, helps the arranger to minimize lost time in writing.

Garcia, Russ. *The Professional Arranger-Composer*
  Volume 1. New York: Criterion Music Corporation, 1954.
  Volume 2. Van Nuys: Alfred Music Publishing, 1979.
   The first volume dates from 1954. It was the first of its kind and the model for texts that followed.

Mancini, Henry. *Sounds and Scores: A Practical Guide to Professional Orchestration*. Van Nuys: Alfred Music Publishing, 1993.
  This truly exceptional book includes a CD with musical examples performed by the author.

Nestico, Sammy. *The Complete Arranger, Revised Edition*. Carlsbad: Fenwood Music Company, 1993.
  A must for the writer's library, Nestico offers advanced coverage of arranging techniques, with valuable introductory pages at the basic level.

Riddle, Nelson. *Arranged by Nelson Riddle: The Definitive Study of Arranging*. Van Nuys: Alfred Music Publishing, 1985.
  This excellent book addresses the best arranging and orchestrating for larger ensembles.

Sebesky, Don: *The Contemporary Arranger*. Van Nuys: Alfred Music Publishing, 1994.
  Sebesky's great book is quite conversational, covering varying ways of scoring as available instrumentation changes from time to time.

Sturm, Fred. *Changes Over Time: The Evolution of Jazz Arranging*. Rottenburg, Germany: Advance Music, 1995.
  This extremely interesting study outlines the growth in jazz arranging over a period of decades.

Sussman, Richard, and Michael Abene. *Jazz Composition and Arranging in the Digital Age*. New York: Oxford University Press, 2012.
  The authors discuss how advances in music technology and software can be integrated with traditional compositional concepts to form a new and more efficient paradigm for the creative process.

Score books and CD recordings by **Maria Schneider** and by trumpeter/flugelhornist **Kenny Wheeler** are also extremely instructive!

The Business of Music

Baskerville, David, and Tim Baskerville. *Music Business Handbook & Career Guide, Edition 9*. Thousand Oaks: Sage Publications, 2010.

> This handbook is considered to be the most comprehensive, up-to-date guide to the music industry and is highly recommended.

Krasilovsky, William, and Sidney Shemel (contributor). *This Business of Music: The Definitive Guide to the Music Industry*. New York: Billboard Books, 2000.

> This valuable resource discusses how to enter — and survive — the music business.

Music Theory and Composition

Adler, Samuel. *The Study of Orchestration, Third Edition*. New York: W.W. Norton & Company, 2002.

> Providing the most comprehensive treatment of both orchestration and instrumentation, this Third Edition retains the elements that have made the book a classic while embracing new technology and responding to the needs of today's students and teachers. Enhanced CDs are included.

Persichetti, Vincent. *Twentieth-Century Harmony: Creative Aspects and Practice*. New York: W.W. Norton & Company, 1961.

> In this now-classic book, the author offers an orderly presentation of the harmonic procedures to be found in music of the first half of the 20th century.

Piston, Walter, and Mark DeVoto. *Harmony, Fifth Edition*. New York: W.W. Norton & Company, 1987.

> The first edition of this text appeared in the early 1940s. It continues to offer an exhaustive treatment of common-practice harmony, the subject of most one- or two-year courses in tonal harmony.

APPENDIX B
HARMONY

Scales and Modes

The C major scale, the C harmonic minor scale, and the C melodic minor scare are given below:

The most common modal scare are shown below, each starting on C. These are influential with the jazz idiom.

Whatever your primary instrument, when you play through these modes, sing them also. By singing them at any tempo, your ear sends creative messages to your brain, expanding your use of these sounds as you write.

Nomenclature

Commonly used **major chords**, with their symbols, are given below.

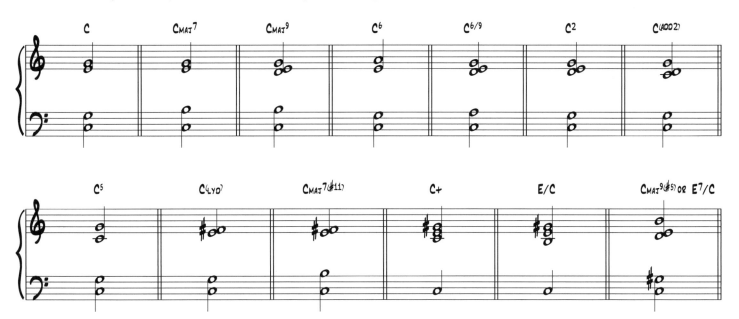

Though the chord symbol shown above is preferred, Cmaj7 is sometimes denoted by these symbols: C△, C△7, Cma7, CM7. It is also important to note that the plain major triad never needs a suffix.

Commonly used **minor chords**, with their symbols, are given below.

Cm7 = also C–7, Cmin7, Cmi7. Of course, this holds true for other minor chords as well.

Compatible Chords

Compatible chords (or "compatibles") are those built from the primary chord's basic scale that can be used when voicing stepwise lines to avoid repeating notes that could cause performance to become awkward.

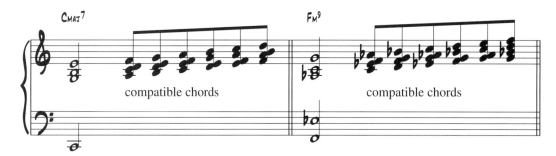

Compatibles are built from many chord types. **Modal** and **half-diminished** are shown below.

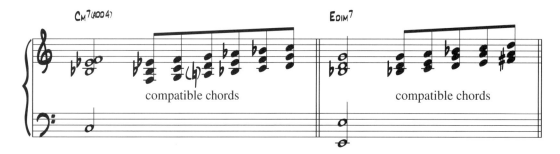

Compatibles and **substitutes** are in the same family. By changing the bass note to a chord, we enter the world of **chord substitution**. In the examples below, the chord symbols above the treble staff are the primaries. Those above the bass notes show the chord after it becomes changed bass. These **changed bass** harmonies frequent a large part of the jazz idiom.

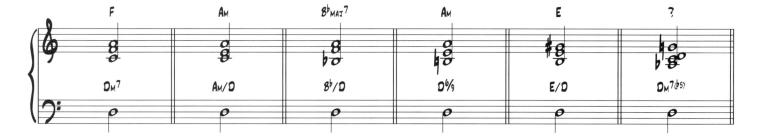

Chord Symbols and MIDI Entry

Chord symbols in computer programs can play "hard to get" at times. Those shown below are concise, and occupy little space. The voicings are contained within one octave, thereby making them playable by one hand on the keyboard when entering chord symbols into a program such as Finale or Sibelius. When such a program refuses to accept the symbol, it's time to teach the program which chord symbols you prefer to use.

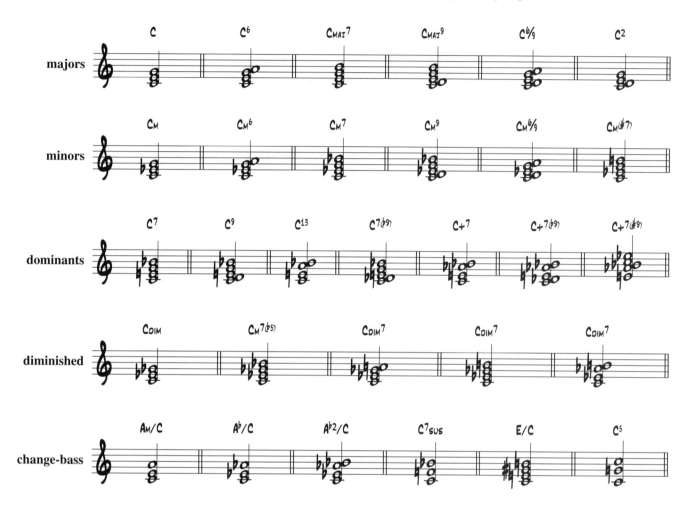

APPENDIX C
THE WIND INSTRUMENTS

Brass – Playing Ranges

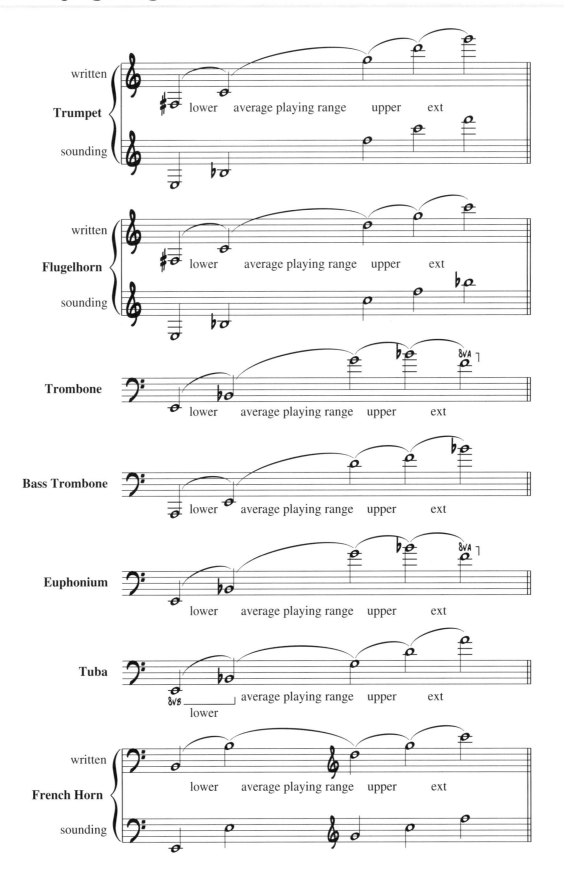

Saxophones – Playing Ranges

The ranges found on these pages show the concert pitches (**sounding**) when a player is given the **written** notes. Finale and Sibelius make these transpositions for us, when the template file is organized properly.

In the Staff column, select Edit Staff Attributes and click/select Transposition. This allows you to choose the transposing key (E♭ for alto and baritone, B♭ for tenor and clarinet).

Saxophone ranges are given below. The first measure shows the written range; the second measure shows the sounding range.

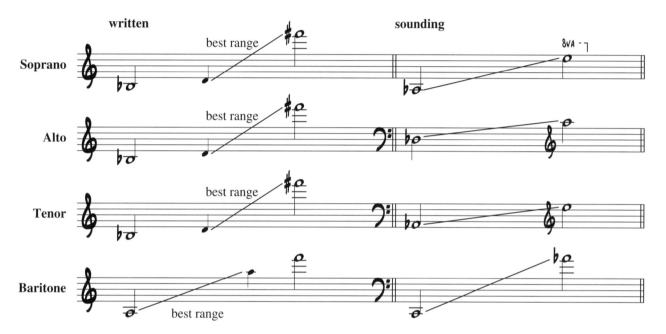

N.B. Most sax players double on one or more woodwind instruments. Before including a doubling instrument in an arrangement, we are wise to discover what doubles are really functional. Also, if both the sax and double are in the same arrangement, when moving on the individual part from a saxophone to the double, be sure that the new transposition and/or clef is shown, with the new key, if and as needed.

Woodwinds – Playing Ranges

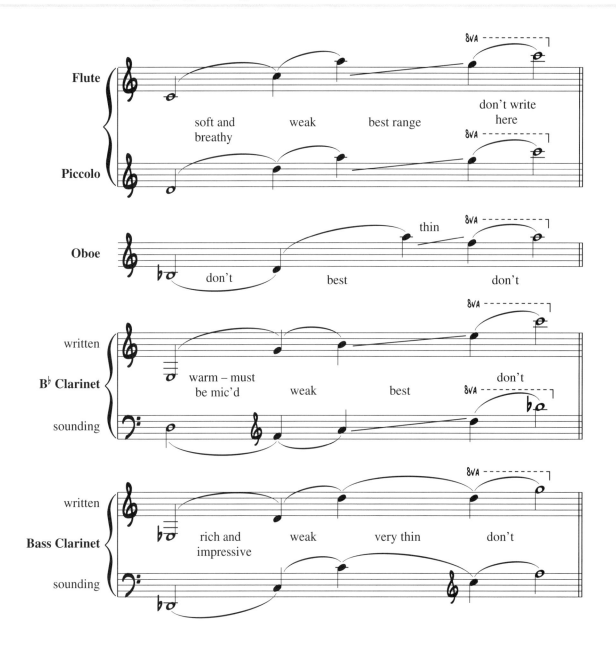

APPENDIX D
THE RHYTHM SECTION

Chapter Seven treats global aspects of the rhythm section — how they relate, the composite rhythm part, individual parts, song form support, and integration. Appendix D will scope the individual instruments as they fit into the styles of jazz and Latin styles. For perspectives on the rhythm section in pop, country, and production styles, see the bibliography on page 68.

Piano and Keyboards

The grand piano (abbr. pf or pno) has the widest range of any acoustical instrument. Soloing falls within the ranges most comfortable to the individual player – the more experienced, the wider the use of the instrument's range.

When comping in a rhythm section, a pianist will avoid the bass range, playing the changes in mid-range or higher, as indicated by style.

When the bass is absent or not playing, the pianist will include bass notes in the playing of changes.

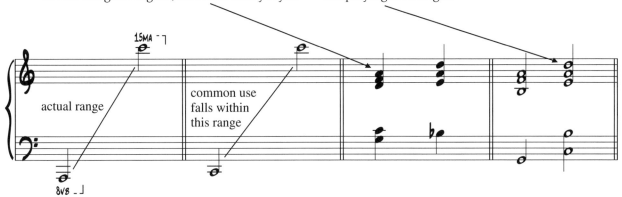

Generic piano parts are usually written on a single staff (either treble or bass) with changes and slash notation (when the style has been set) or with rhythm notation (when specifics are needed).

Let rhythm players know who's playing, and give **simple instructions** (in English) to help them play sensitively as early as possible. Rhythm parts lacking this information force the player into a cautious pattern while learning the arrangement. This slows the rehearsal process, or compromises a sight-reading performance, thus embarrassing the player.

Improvised solos...   **...are brought to a close this way:**

Specifically written parts are appropriate 1) when *ad lib* comping would complicate the rhythmic content of the ensemble, and 2) when required by a director or publisher. Specific parts should be easily read, and never as complicated as if the music were being played *ad lib*.

In the example below, the complexity of notated music would require advance rehearsal or practice to avoid mistakes when in ensemble. When you need such sounds, be sure that the advance preparation or rehearsal is possible.

****

As seen in the following example, chord symbols placed above specifically written music help the jazz player quickly interpret what is to be played while, at the same time, listening to the rest of the rhythm section for style and togetherness. Music lacking these helpers can cause unnecessary error. Unless you are sure of your player and know that he/she has time to scope the music before rehearsing, keep the rhythmic complexity at a low level when writing specific piano voicings.

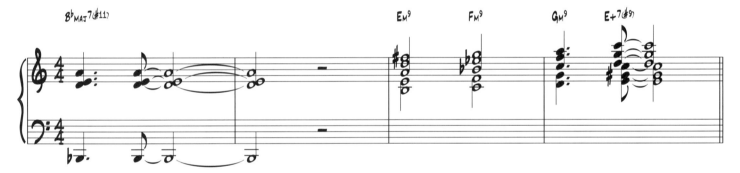

Notice in bars 3–4 above that music written with opposing stems suggests two-hand playing, even though written on only one staff. This is more easily read than on two staves with change of clef.

****

Under special circumstances, the arranger is required to specifically notate an entire piano part. These circumstances include published charts to be performed by young bands and music for the stage. Check with the publisher!

Specific parts should be easily read, and should contain fewer notes than one would expect from a player whose comping is entirely spontaneous. The most important requirement for such writing is that of simplicity, but never at the expense of the style and idiom of the chart. When the need for such writing arises, start by checking out a few published charts.

INNER THOUGHTS

By Paris Rutherford

Three guidelines are followed in this piano part:

- When no chord symbols appear, this is a signal that the arranger expects the music to be played exactly as written. When chord symbols are there as well, the pianist is free to adjust things to his/her ear and technique.

- Rhythmic lines (bars 6 and 7) are followed by a sustain, to let the rest of the rhythm section respond to complete the feeling.

- Ranges and voicing types agree entirely with "Arranger's Piano."

The Bass

The bass instrument in jazz is either an acoustic upright contrabass (abbr: Bass) or its contemporary counterpart, the electric bass (abbr: El Bs). These abbreviations are used only to identify the bass line on page 2 and onward in a score. Both acoustic and electric bass are concert-pitched, transposing instruments that read exclusively the bass clef.

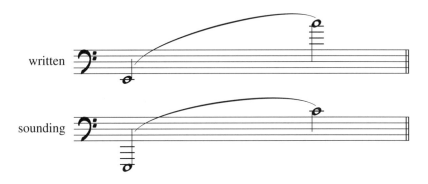

In **classical music**, the bass (contrabass) is bowed (*arco*) unless specified pizzicato (*pizz*). In **jazz**, just the opposite: acoustic bass (bass) is pizzicato unless asked to bow (*arco*). The electric bass is entirely pizzicato.

The line of music played by the bass instrument, whether acoustic or electric, forms the basis for the harmonic content of any arrangement, whatever style. For this reason, bass is commonly referred to as the **cornerstone** of the harmonic structure existing within the arrangement. When we write a bass line, it must be a good one! Otherwise, the arrangement suffers.

Written Bass Lines

Write the bass line where the bass needs to play specific notes, to be stylistically in keeping with the band or just the rest of the section. Then use chord symbols with an instruction such as "continue" or "etc." The bass line found in the example below is from "Upstairs." The full score is in Appendix E. The recording is on CD Track 1.

Example: "Upstairs"

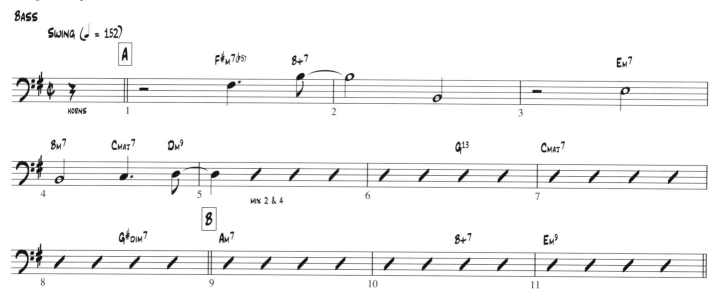

Under normal circumstances, two to four bars of written music followed by chord changes allows the bassist to play in the desired style without having endless written lines. When the line is written later, though, the player knows how to approach the written bass successfully.

This is an excerpt from "The Blues" (score in Appendix E, recording on CD Track 15). Note the tempo head "Swing Mix," which tells the player to use a looser mix of swing two and four, never staying totally "in two."

Example: "The Blues"

While the bass is capable of melody, double stops (two notes played simultaneously), and special effects, the primary function of the bass in the jazz arrangement (or composition) is to keep stylistic time and to provide the foundation for the rhythm section.

Bassist and drummer alike require style information and desired tempo, along with cues to show both players where the important horn figures are located. For both rhythm players, these are entered as cues into the part, usually on the top of the staff, in layer three (Finale and Sibelius) so that the stems remain facing upward.

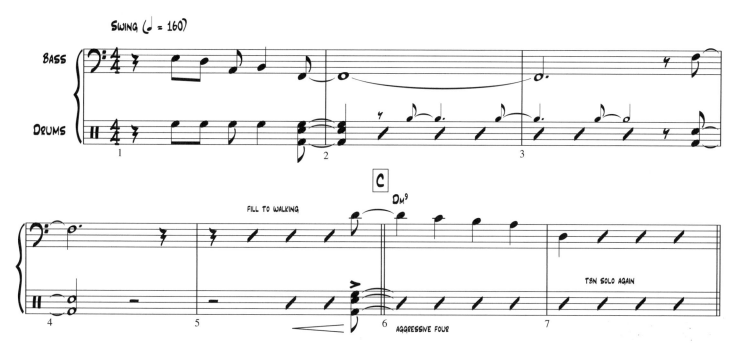

Writing for Drums

Drum parts are written according to style and also to the experience level of the player. In addition to these parameters, some publishers expect more detail on parts they believe may be played by beginners. In such cases, more experienced players choose to smile and accept what they are given without feeling compromised.

The drum part is written with a **drum clef**, also known as a **neutral clef** (two vertical lines). Notating in Finale or Sibelius, the drum clef can receive information according either to treble or bass clef entry, whichever is more convenient to the arranger. Style instructions in English (or any desired language) are usually placed above the music, sometimes below if readability would be improved. In early attempts to write for drums, it is important that the writer communicates with an experienced drummer to validate the style being used on the drum part.

Drum parts with **specific notation** are laid out according to the following:

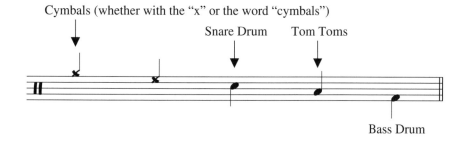

In jazz arrangements, specific notation is generally limited to a few bars to set the style (or for full ensemble sounds), followed then by slash notation with downsized cues as needed.

Swing-Jazz Style

Examples here are for music in the swing-jazz style. Other styles will be shown later.

When the style is swing-four, the notation below is standard for young players.

Normally, though, the notation below (with instructions) is adequate for showing the swing-four style. Drummers will keep cymbal time with one hand and add little fills with the other. The use of the bass drum depends on tempo and the complexity of the chart.

Drum parts should be easy to read without have to keep one's eyes totally fixed on the music. Numbers in parentheses help the drummer listen to the group and catch the horn stabs in bars 27 and 28. These horn cues are entered into Layer 3, which (one hopes) will automatically point stems upward.

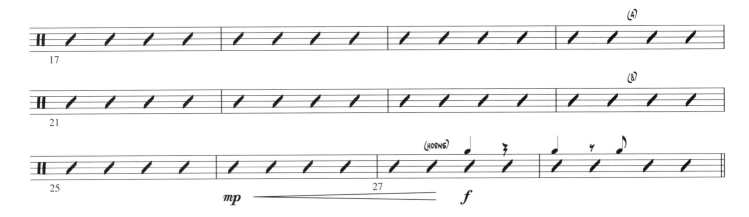

Eighth Styles

Examples are given now for styles that are not in swing, such as bossa nova, straight eight, etc. In all of these "eighth styles," a faster tempo requires less cue notation, while slower tempos may require more. In all drum parts, whatever the style or tempo, dynamics are very important.

Bossa Nova

Bossa nova has a characteristic two-measure rhythm, with a pulse of either 2:3 or 3:2, depending upon the motion within the tune itself. Drum parts for both sub-styles can be written either of these two ways, depending on the experience level of the drummer.

As mentioned earlier, the drum part layout will be written with sufficient notation to establish the sound needed for the arrangement, including "catches" for horn work, but without overwriting.

Other Straight-Eight Styles

In addition to Latin styles (bossa nova, mambo, etc.) other straight-eight styles are heard and felt in much of today's jazz-influenced music. These styles range from soft and transparent to hardcore and aggressive. Drum parts are written with a combination of notes and instructions, as seen in the next two examples, recordings for which are found on the CD.

This excerpt from "The Front" (CD Track 19) is in a soft and transparent eight style. It includes both notation and instructions.

Example: "The Front"

This example comes from CD Track 3, "Traveling." It is an aggressive eight style called "Street," to suggest a similarity to the New Orleans Street Beat.

Example: "Traveling"

N.B. "Street Beat" is the fundamental basis for most modern and aggressive rhythm styles. The patterns usually heard closely resemble those in the following example:

Afro-Cuban Drum Patterns

Shown below are typical drum patterns for five most-used Afro-Cuban styles. Note that two (bossa nova and salsa) can be fashioned in two ways, depending upon the melodic motion. In both, the bass and bass drum are always together on the important beats, even though the bass will be playing more notes according to the energy of the chart.

Further Resources

For a complete coverage of drum patterns and styles, check out the following:

Afro-Cuban Rhythms for Drumset by Frank Malabe & Bob Weiner (Alfred Music Publishing, 1990).

A well-constructed introduction to drum and percussion rhythms for Afro-Cuban styles; the included CD is a valuable learning tool.

Out On All Limbs, Volumes 1 and 2 by Mike Drake (self-published, 2013).

Here you will discover a complete list of the drum patterns found in jazz, rock, pop, and Latin styles. CDs are included. Available at www.mikedrakemusic.com.

The Jazz Guitar

Guitar is perhaps the most colorful member of the rhythm section. While there are several models of the instrument, the most commonly used in jazz is the solid body with steel strings. The guitar will be amplified, the amplifier placed next to (or immediately behind) the player, who normally adjusts the sounds and volume according to the need.

The guitar has six strings, is written in the treble clef, and sounds an octave lower than written.

It has a sounding range as shown here:

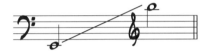

Due to its colorful sound, the guitar can contribute several additives to the arrangement:

- When comping, guitar is given the same style information as others in the rhythm section.

Example: "Traveling"

- Guitar can be given specific notes, usually joining others in the group. In "The Blues" (Appendix E and CD Track 15), the guitar is given specific notes with the rest of the rhythm section in bars 5–12, then unison with the tenor sax at Letter A. (Guitar is written one octave higher to create a unison sound.)
- When one of the rhythm section instruments drops out for a section, the effect is very noticeable, and therefore a good arranging technique. Check out the following:
    1. In "Turning One #2," the guitar drops out during the piano solo, second time at A.
    2. In "The Front," the piano drops out at letter D and the guitar comps the tenor sax solo.

Most arrangers today write for guitar as they do for bass and drums. Except where specific notation is required, two to four bars of specific rhythms can be followed by slash notation, chord symbols, and instructions as needed.

APPENDIX E
SCORES

CD Track List

Track	Title
1	Upstairs – demo
2	Upstairs – rhythm section only
3	Traveling – demo
4	Traveling – rhythm section only
5	Porch Time – demo
6	Porch Time – rhythm section only
7	Turning One #1 – demo
8	Turning One #1 – rhythm section only
9	Turning One # 2 – demo
10	Turning One #2 – rhythm section only
11	Turning One #2 – original demo (Logic)
12	Turning Two – demo
13	Turning Two – rhythm section only
14	Turning Two – horns alone, from bridge out
15	The Blues – demo
16	The Blues – rhythm section only
17	Inner Thoughts – demo
18	Inner Thoughts – rhythm section only
19	The Front – demo
20	The Front – rhythm section only
21	The Front – with vocal
22	Together – demo
23	Together – rhythm section only

UPSTAIRS

By Paris Rutherford

UPSTAIRS

By Paris Rutherford

TRAVELING

By Paris Rutherford

TRAVELING

By Paris Rutherford

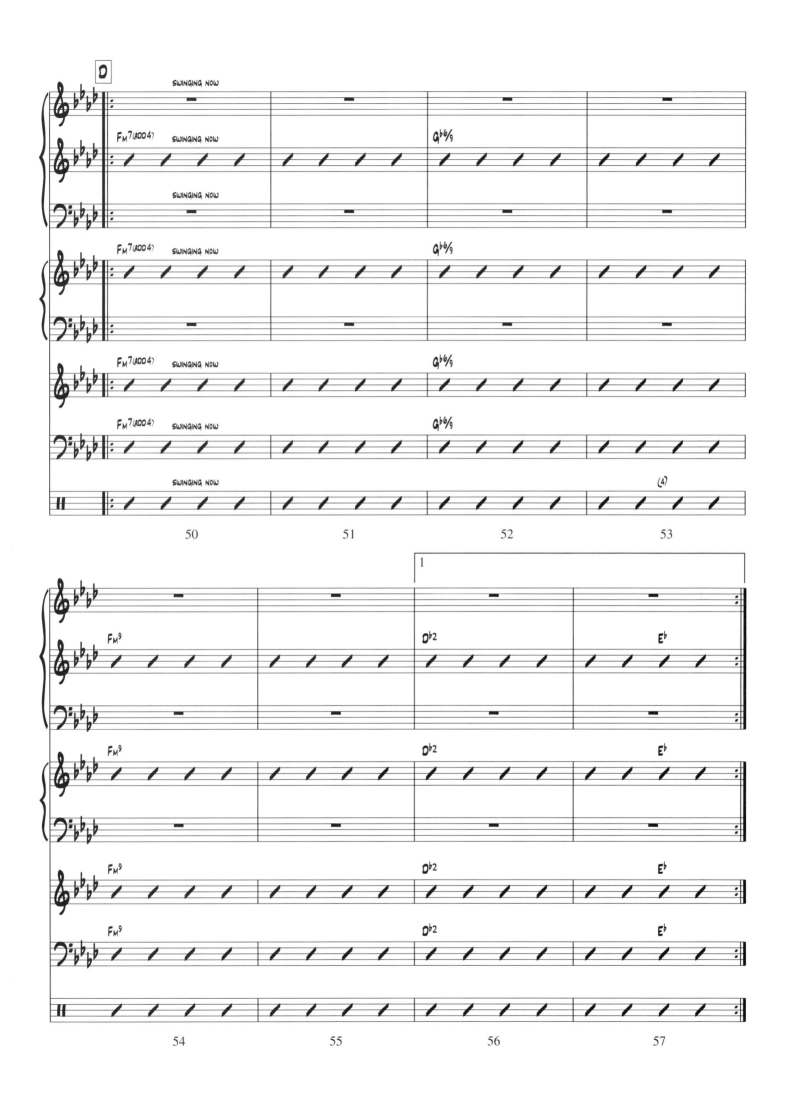

PORCH TIME

By Paris Rutherford

PORCH TIME

By Paris Rutherford

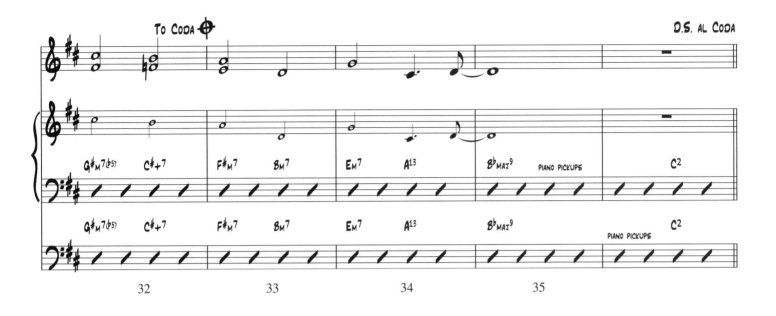

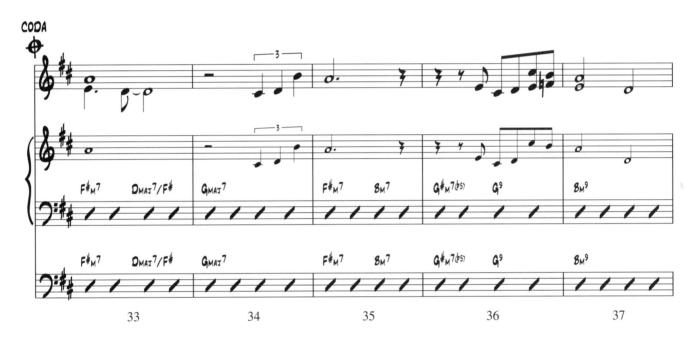

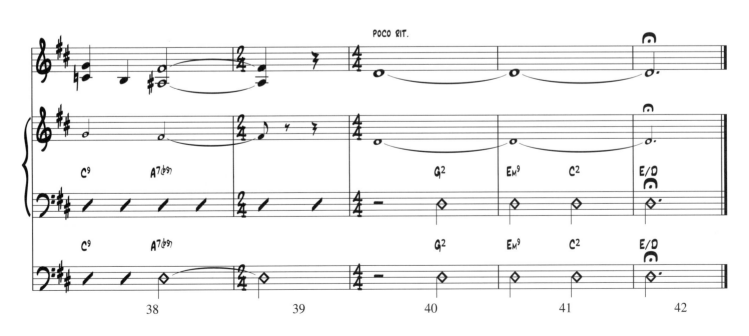

TURNING ONE #1 (ABAB)

By Paris Rutherford

TURNING ONE #2 (ABAB)

By Paris Rutherford

SCORE

Score pages are redesigned to save space. Normally they are full, as on page one.

TURNING TWO (AABA)

By Paris Rutherford

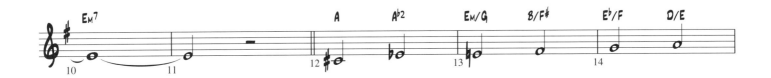

TURNING TWO (AABA)

By Paris Rutherford

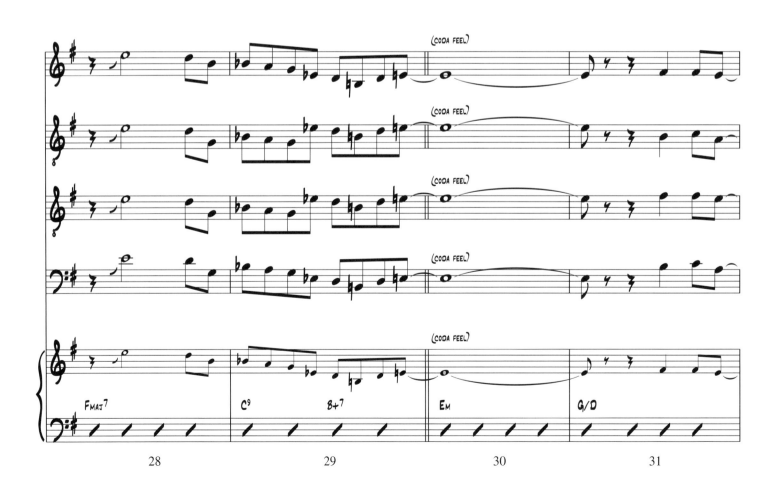

THE BLUES

By Paris Rutherford

THE BLUES

By Paris Rutherford

INNER THOUGHTS

By Paris Rutherford

INNER THOUGHTS

By Paris Rutherford

SCORE

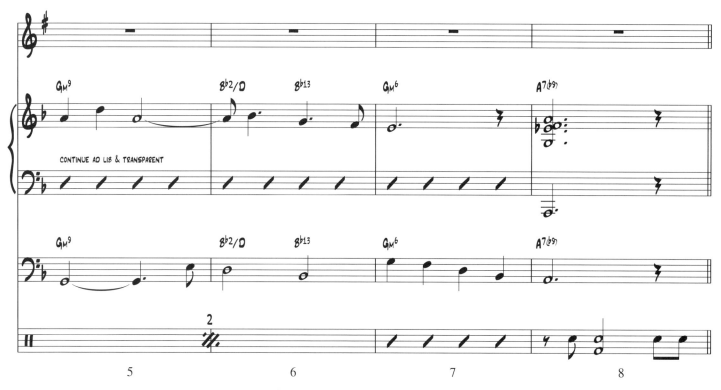

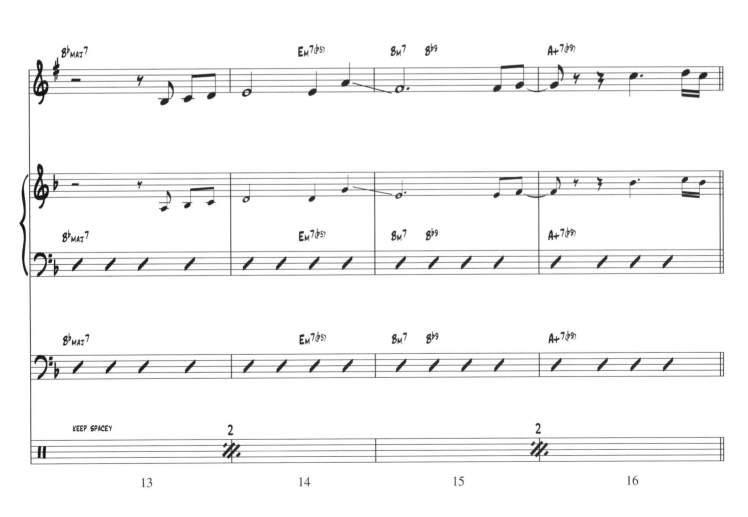

THE FRONT

By Paris Rutherford

THE FRONT

Music by Paris Rutherford
Arranged by P. Milton

TOGETHER

Music and Lyrics by
Paris Rutherford